# ADVANCE PRAISE

"Flow state is a coveted goal of all endurance athletes, including mountaineers. The habits described here are directly applicable to ascending all of the peaks of life."
**Tom French**
Everest summiteer

"Max Landsberg has crafted a wonderful fusion of Eastern and Western thinking to offer insights and habits for living in productive harmony with each other and the cosmos".
**Alice Au**
Board Member and co-lead of Asia Pacific Board and CEO Practice, Spencer Stuart.

"This excellent book shows the everyday habits that can help us live in tune with the cosmos, each other, and ultimately ourselves."
**Vlatko Vedral**
Professor of Quantum Information Theory, University of Oxford

"Engaging, enjoyable and actionable. *The Power of the Dao* playfully distils ancient wisdom into practical actions for today's world."
**Paul Willmott**
Chief Digital Advisor, LEGO Brand Group

"Max offers insight into challenging ideas and practical steps to apply them in our over-busy lives."

**Keith Leslie**
Chair of Samaritans


"This book is a great read. It shows how you can engage with nature and your environment in an authentic way, and the great benefits in doing so."

**Doug Gurr**
Director, The Natural History Museum.


"Flow is a gift we can give ourselves. This book shows how."

**Professor David Clutterbuck**
Special Ambassador, European Mentoring and Coaching Council


"In this era of extraordinary disruption, never has there been a greater need for leaders to achieve 'Flow' and the book that Max has written is about the best guide you could wish for."

**Humphrey Cobbold**
CEO, PureGym


"If you want to learn the seven habits to living a more fulfilling life, this is the book for you. In it, you'll find a treasure trove of tools to thrive in a challenging world".

**Dr. Declan Woods**
Professor of Leadership Practice, King's College London and CEO, teamGenie®

## PRAISE FOR *THE TAO OF COACHING*

"Great coaches in sport and business are made not born, and they make themselves by thinking, planning, listening and systematically building their skills. In this book the great coaches of tomorrow have found exactly where to start their journey."

**David Kirk**
Captain of the 1987 World Champion All Blacks rugby team


"I'm making this useful guide required reading for my executive team."

**George Farr**
Vice-Chairman, American Express Company


## PRAISE FOR *MASTERING COACHING*

"This is a genuinely good book, elegantly exemplifying its own messages: Max Landsberg doesn't tell us what to do, but illuminates the reasons for doing what we already know we should."

**Jonathan Gosling**
Professor of Leadership, University of Exeter


"Max cuts mercilessly through the guff, to distil the best of the insights, tools and science we need to be world-class coaches, leaders and friends, right now."

**Anne Scoular**
Founder, Meyler Campbell

Published by
**LID Publishing**
An imprint of LID Business Media Ltd.
LABS House, 15-19 Bloomsbury Way,
London, WC1A 2TH, UK

info@lidpublishing.com
www.lidpublishing.com

A member of:

businesspublishersroundtable.com

© Max Landsberg, 2023
© LID Business Media Limited, 2023

Printed by Gutenberg Press, Malta
ISBN: 978-1-911687-74-0
ISBN: 978-1-911687-75-7 (ebook)

Cover and page design: Caroline Li

This book is dedicated to
Roxana Donath

# THE
# POWER
## OF THE
# DAO

Seven Essential Habits for Living in
**Flow**, **Fulfilment** and **Resilience**

**Max Landsberg**

MADRID | MEXICO CITY | LONDON
BUENOS AIRES | BOGOTA | SHANGHAI

# CONTENTS

# ATTAINING THE DAO TO LIVE IN FLOW

*(Seeing a clear way forward. The key principles of Daoism.
Where this book comes from. This book's structure.
Using this book.)*

Of my several near-fatal accidents, the happiest (or at least the most enlightening) was when I was nearly killed by a pizza.

Three decades ago, when I was still a workaholic, I had been working at home one Friday evening ... while also watching TV and eating that pizza. I had not been concentrating on any one of those activities. A sharp pain suddenly pierced my throat. I sipped some water, but the pain got worse. I drank another sip; the pain ratcheted up. I glanced down at that pizza and, to my horror, saw not a splinter of wood ... but half a splinter. A throat inflammation can quickly suffocate you. So in quick succession there was the ambulance to the emergency room, the general anaesthetic, the endoscopic removal of the other half of the splinter, and a weekend in hospital recovering with a drip in my arm.

A friend gave me a book to read while I recuperated. It introduced me to Daoism, the insights of which would have a huge influence on my life. The techniques of Daoism helped me write a book that has sold more than a million copies. They gave me simple advice that I could offer to the hundreds of clients whom I would later coach over three decades. More holistically, they stopped me from being a workaholic and helped me live in 'flow,' fulfilment and balance most of the time.

This book aims to offer up those insights in a simple and practical way, so you can see a clear way forward and live in flow, even as the world's kaleidoscope of change swivels ever faster. Using Daoist principles, you can access the state of flow for extended periods. This in turn can help you solve your daily problems, make the most of your opportunities, and help the people you are coaching or leading live a richer life.

This book presents seven habits that will let you achieve this. Each habit is anchored robustly in one of the enduring principles of Daoism. Over thousands of years, these principles and habits have led to improved performance, fulfilment and resilience. For each habit I offer three succinct maxims and stories, to act as prompts as you develop and live these habits.

## SEEING A CLEAR WAY FORWARD

Being in flow is when you are 'in the zone.' You are 'on your game,' or even 'on fire.' This is both a mental state and a physical one. You have a feeling of complete focus, full involvement and deep enjoyment in whatever you are doing. You are utterly absorbed. You are resourceful and resilient. Things are effortless: your activities take no energy from you – indeed, they give energy to you. You barely notice the passage of time. You feel calm yet almost ecstatic.

You may have glimpsed being in this state of flow – when hitting the perfect tennis shot, cracking the egg perfectly with no loose bits of shell, cracking the perfect joke. But it is indeed possible to be in this zone not just for a moment of flow, nor merely for a day of flow, but always and forever.

Much of the secret of reaching this state lies in seven habits. These start by developing your ability to see or sense the unvarnished truth of your surroundings in a clear and unblinkered way. This is the promise of Daoism. That promise is symbolized by the very word for *Dao* in Chinese:

道

This character has two parts. On the left, 辶 means 'walk.' On the right, 首 means 'head.' So, the symbol 道 'Dao' implies 'to go ahead.'[1] As with most Chinese characters, it contains further undercurrents and meanings, woven into this single picture. For example, the character for head also means chief or first (as 'head' coincidentally does in English too: head chef, head teacher). And the rectangle in the centre of the head is an eye. So, the Dao character also suggests 'the chief way forward,' and even 'seeing the way forward.'

The stories presented throughout this book show you how to find and use this clear-sightedness. This can lead you to deliver virtuoso performance more consistently – and live in the type of flow set out in Mihaly Csikszentmihalyi's foundational 1990 book *Flow: The Psychology of Optimal Experience*. This can also give you greater fulfilment and resilience.

---

1   See Wieger, *Chinese Characters: Their Origin, Etymology, History, Classification, and Signification*, p 789 for 'going and pausing' and p 326 for 'go ahead.'

# THE KEY PRINCIPLES OF DAOISM

Daoism is a set of principles and habits that help you live more in tune with the world. It favours simple beliefs and practices over commandments, and it offers new mindsets rather than detailed prescriptions and instructions.

Daoist thinking and practices emerged in China 3,000 years ago. In Western terms, it is a rich cocktail that includes the simple Stoic principles of Ancient Greece. It mixes in, however, the joyousness and spontaneity of the hippies. Early Daoists did not belong to religious institutions, and they rejected complex theories. Thus Daoism is not really a religion. Some people consider it a philosophy; if so, it's an extremely practical one.

Before looking in detail at each principle and its related habit, let's take a quick look at the underlying mindset on which they are based. (I use the word 'cosmos' quite often in this book. I intend this to mean not 'stars and galaxies,' but everything that is going on in the world. Similarly, by 'nature' I do not mean merely 'trees and bees' but everything going on in the world. I therefore use the following terms interchangeably: cosmos, world, nature, ecosystem, environment, etc).

The Daoist mindset includes several core beliefs: the cosmos is a connected ecosystem; change is continuous and pervasive; we are better working *with* the dynamics of our team, family or environment rather than thinking we are smart enough to 'push the river' and substantially go against the cosmos; self-development is a worthwhile venture that often means discarding assumptions in order to see the past, present and future with greater clarity and simplicity.

At its heart, Daoism aims to encourage your own energy to act in synergy with the energy of your surroundings and the cosmos. We call this pervasive energy *qi* 气 (pronounced 'chee') in Chinese.[2] This vital force is inherent in everything. As Einstein observed in his theory of relativity: $E = mc^2$!

*Qi* is also a central factor in traditional Chinese medicine and Chinese martial arts. You may be familiar with them from their influence on the practices of tai chi and qigong.

Below are the seven principles and habits that can best help us live in flow. Daoism, of course, has many additional principles. But for this book I have selected a manageably small number of these principles to serve as an introduction. I present them sequentially to create the best journey for your exploration and discovery. You will, however, see that most of these principles are strongly related to each other.

You can use the diagram below as a guide as you develop your understanding and intentional practice. To simplify, the first three principles, starting with *yin-yang* at the centre, are about the way that you and your environment work. These include: Flows of potential energies, Patterns, and Natural self-so-ness[3]). The next three principles are more about how you choose to interact with your environment. These include Simplicity, Effortless action, and Potency. The last principle is where you end up 'attaining the Dao' (Mastery). By attaining the Dao you are able to live your whole life in flow.

----

2    The simplified character 气 comes from an ancient character that showed a link between the three horizontal lines of Heaven, Mankind and Earth. The traditional character 氣 shows steam rising above rice 米. As rice combines the idea of low, watery *yin* and high, sunny *yang*, the traditional character suggests the flow of energy from *yin* and *yang*. The new, simplified character is said to represent steam from a sacrifice rising energetically upwards.

3    We explore the 'self-so-ness' aspect of spontaneity in the chapters on *ziran*.

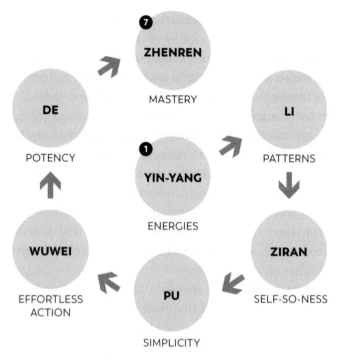

**MAP OF THE SEVEN PRINCIPLES**

These principles and their related habits will be explored in detail in later chapters. As a high-level summary, however:

1. *Yin* and *yang*, as characterized by the well-known symbol ☯, represent complementary forces in the environment, such as good/bad, active/passive, etc. These forces are in continuous and interrelated flux. By being able to habitually sense the *yin* and *yang* in a situation, you can better sense how energies are flowing, and see the opportunities and threats that you might otherwise overlook.

2. *Li* means patterns. By recognizing the patterns in people, situations and nature, you can gain a better view of how and when to use the undercurrents of the cosmos in your favour.

3. **Ziran** is hard to translate, but means the 'natural self-so-ness' of how the cosmos (including people) typically behaves. By staying in tune with this, you can act in concert with things, and avoid unintended consequences.

4. **Pu** means simplicity and clarity: sensing the world in an uncomplicated way. As we will see, you can get there by using meditation to 'fast the heart-mind,' and dissolving your biases by 'sweeping the lodging house' of your spirit. *Pu* helps you observe and interpret *yin-yang, li* and *ziran* more truthfully, and to understand your environment with great clarity and accuracy.

5. **Wuwei** means effortless action. By mastering this, you cultivate your energies, rather than frittering them away in stratagems that are too contrived. It can generate moments of being 'in flow.'

6. **De** means potency. It is how you act in ways authentic to yourself and to the prior five principles. When you act in tune with your *de*, you radiate an attractive power that draws people and serendipity to you.

7. **Zhenren** means mastery. This is mastery of yourself-as-connected-with-the-cosmos. It is what allows you to live a life that is in flow all the time. In the words of the Daoist book *Zhuangzi* (and repeated by martial artist and movie legend Bruce Lee) you will:

> "Moving, be like water.
> Still, be like a mirror.
> Respond like an echo."

You can apply these principles in any situation. By following them in a regular, habitual way, millions of people have lived better, happier and more productive lives. A long list of eminent people have embraced them. This includes philosophers such as Martin Heidegger, Immanuel Kant,

Arthur Schopenhauer and Bertrand Russell; writers such as Leo Tolstoy, Henry David Thoreau, Ralph Waldo Emerson and Oscar Wilde; psychologists such as Carl Jung and Abraham Maslow; architects such as Frank Lloyd Wright; songwriters from George Harrison to rapper RZA; Nobel laureates such as Niels Bohr and Tu Youyou, who in 2015 became the first Chinese woman to win the Nobel Prize; and even Bruce Lee and Steve Jobs.

## THE STORIES

This book brings each of these principles – and their related habits – to life through *chengyu* stories.

*Chengyu* are Chinese sayings. They are maxims like the English 'every cloud has a silver lining,' except that the *chengyu* typically have deeper meanings. They often have a backstory that further embellishes the gist. For example, one of the *chengyu* to illustrate *li* (patterns) is *Old Frontiersman Loses Horse*. The story is only a page long, but it deepens our understanding, and makes it more memorable. These stories, and their *chengyu* titles help convert the concise maxim into a trigger to pop up and remind you of its main meaning when needed.

Other *chengyu* we explore include *Brush Stops, Meaning Continues*; *Pierce Wall, Steal Light*; *Eight Immortals Cross the Sea*; and *Legs Akimbo, Practically Naked*.

With remarkable economy, most of these *chengyu* are just four characters long (in Chinese!).

# WHERE THIS BOOK COMES FROM

During 30 years of coaching hundreds of successful leaders, managers and experts, I realized a pattern. I noticed that the principles and practices of the Daoists, in which I had long held an interest, were highly relevant for personal development. They also offered uniquely valuable signposts for the broader quest to 'live in flow.' Their lack of dogma makes them very attractive to the modern heart-mind.

I searched for a guidebook to give to my clients. It would offer up the essence of the Daoist way. It would present the advice clearly, and with a practical bent. I found many academic works that were scholarly but abstruse. I found other books and articles that merely recounted the history of the Daoist way. I found some books that came close to what I sought, and I cite them in the following pages. But I failed to find a guidebook that spoke to me with the mix that I sought of conceptual rigor and clear usability.

This is the book that I had failed to find. It draws from four main sources. Firstly, it is based on my own 30 years' experience of coaching many hundreds of people. As a partner or senior partner at one of the world's top business consulting firms, and at two of the world's top executive search firms, I have been privileged to coach a wide range of people. In these roles, I developed a passion for helping people become more effective in their jobs, and also more at ease with themselves and their worlds. I found that most people can learn to become more successful in their jobs. But I noticed that relatively few people manage to achieve this success while also living in flow. I took a strong interest in how those latter people accomplished that.

Secondly, the content of this book comes from a deep study of the daily practices of Daoism. In the 25 years since

I wrote the million-copy-selling guide *The Tao of Coaching*,[4] I have studied Daoism in depth. I have explored the Daoist mountains of China on foot, and have tried to live as a Daoist of sorts.

The third source of content is the *chengyu* maxims and stories. I first read of them in my hospital bed, after the near-deadly pizza.

Finally, I included material from five principal texts of Daoism. First is **Daodejing** (meaning *The Classic of the Way and [Its] Power*). You may know it as *Dao De Jing or Tao Te Ching*. It is a collection of verses from around 300 BCE. It is traditionally attributed to a man named Laozi, meaning 'the old master,' though it more likely derives from multiple sources. Second is **Zhuangzi**, named after Zhuang Zhou – a thinker and aristocrat who died in 286 BCE. The work is a compilation from various authors, dating from 5th-3rd century BCE. Third is **Liezi**, also known as *The True Classic of the Perfect Virtue of Simplicity and Emptiness*. It is a compilation of pithy stories named after a sage who may or may not have existed. Fourth is **Neiye** (meaning *Inward Training*). This dates from the 4th century BCE. It is one of the earliest Chinese texts to focus on breathing, meditation and the circulation of the vital energy, *qi*. The fifth foundational text is the far older **Yijing** (*Book of Changes*, aka *I Ching*).

Each of these texts has its own character, as you will see. *Zhuangzi* and *Liezi*, in particular, tell succinct stories in engaging prose. They are worth a read. The Further Reading section describes these books in more detail.

---

4  Dao is a more contemporary rendering of 'Tao.'

## THIS BOOK'S STRUCTURE

Each part of this book addresses one of the seven principles set out above.

I first explain the principle in detail, including where and why to notice it, and then show techniques for developing awareness of it and applying it as a habit.

Three short stories in successive chapters then illuminate important nuances of the principle. Each story is headed by a *chengyu* maxim, as explained above. I have also included several contemporary stories to highlight the current relevance of the principles.

Each story aims to take you on an adventure. You will discover memorable tips, tweaks of mindset, and mini-mantras that you can adopt and can pass on to others. These can help you live more fully and creatively.

To help you digest and apply the learnings, each chapter ends with a brief summary and suggestions for reflective learning.

---

This guide focuses on the practical lessons of classical Daoism, not on its later religious additions. The early Daoists advocated freedom of thinking (in part as a reaction to the growing strictures of Confucianism). They rejected dogma. Yet within a few centuries, hierarchies of priests, canons and libraries had emerged – the very complexity that the early Daoists had avoided. This book focuses on the former 'practical philosophy,' rather than the later 'religion.' That said, many of Daoism's later developments, such as the inclusion of Confucian and Buddhist principles, may be of interest and value to you. I therefore outline these developments in Appendix 1.

# USING THIS BOOK, AND THE YIN-YANG NEEDLE

The goal of this book is not to convert you into being a full-time Daoist. Rather, it offers you a lens through which you can see the world, and your interactions with it, in new and valuable ways. Even if you can tap into just a few of the habits suggested, you can gain the immediate benefits of focus, calmness and creativity. If you can live all of the principles *continuously*, then your world will be a far better place.

Finally, this book is not a recipe book of instructions or a workbook in which the reader is meant to do most of the work; it is, however, a mix of these two genres.

Let me explain. As I was writing this book, it struck me that *any* book should be like a *yin-yang* needle. As we explore shortly, *yin* can represent 'receptivity,' while *yang* can represent 'activity.' The words, ideas and statements in a book are thus like the active *yang* tip of the needle. But equally important is the receptive *yin* eye of the needle. The eye of the needle is a portal through which you can thread your own meaning, values and relevance. Once you have threaded the needle, you can pull it through the fabric of your own life. In other words: you will get the most out of this book if you follow at least some of the suggested reflections, and experiment with putting the insights you develop into practice.

You can gain the benefits of the Daoist way using any of three approaches:

- Picking out several habits to adopt that can help you right now in your daily life.
- Tweaking your mindset to see more fully the value of working in tune with your cosmos, by quite literally co—operating with it.

- Reinforcing your own grasp of Daoism, as a leader or coach, by helping your team, family or friends to discover the power of the Dao.

陰陽

yin yang

# PRINCIPLE 1

# YIN-YANG
## (ENERGIES)

SENSE THE ENERGIES ...
TO BETTER SEE OPPORTUNITIES AND THREATS

This chapter explains *yin* and *yang*. It then shows where you can discern them, and the benefits of doing so. It also illustrates how you can develop your sense of *yin-yang* in your daily life. You will find the *yin-yang* principle woven through much of the Daoist way.

For the Daoist, everything has the qualities of both *yin* and *yang*. *Yin* and *yang* are characteristics, not substances. You can think of them as the blackness and whiteness that exist in various degrees of greyness. Situations, things and even people have both *yin* and *yang* traits, as we shall see.

The *yang* characteristic is often described as positive. Translations of *yang* include 'bright, glorious; open out, expand.' Its Chinese character is a useful signpost to its wider meanings. *Yang* is 陽, which combines the symbol for a hill, rotated sideways (阝) and the symbol for the sunny side (昜). So, *yang* means bright and also evident, explicable, patent, purposeful and positive.

In contrast, *yin* 陰 is the shaded side (佘) of the hill (阝). So *yin* stands for the characteristics of shaded, hidden, mysterious, latent, receptive and negative.

Crucially, *yin* and *yang* are not opposites that exclude each other; rather, they complement each other in a dynamic way. The hill symbolism helps us here. One side of the hill is bright because of the positive *yang* illumination of the sun. The other side is dark because of the *yin* lack of sunlight. So as the sky turns from night to day, it is the shift from *yin* to *yang* that creates the energy flows on the ground. Anyone who has camped near the foot of a hill will have felt the morning breeze rise up the hill, and the evening breeze flow down it. For a simpler analogy, you could think of *yin* and *yang* as the two sides of the coin that is *qi* (vital force).

As shown in the well-known symbol of *yin-yang*, the *tai-jitu* symbol ☯, Daoists see the world as composed of change that is both continuous and interrelated. Daoists are keenly aware of the energies driving that change, which is powered by the interplay between receptive *yin* and animated *yang*. Nothing is absolutely at rest; rest is merely an intermediate state of movement, or latent movement, which is pregnant with possibility.

Daoists know they will be happier and more fulfilled if they adapt to the changes in circumstances that are powered by *yin* and *yang*, and advance with the times.

This stands in contrast to typical Western philosophy. In the West, we often focus on achieving specific states, with change seen as a way to get from one state to another. Even though Heraclitus pointed out that you 'can't put your foot in the same river twice,' he did not explain clearly how to live and work with that idea. Daoism does.

The *yin* and *yang* in a situation are often obvious: positive-negative; purposeful-reflective; push-pull. Sometimes the dynamic is less obvious: conscious-subconscious;

health-unwellness; poverty-wealth; before we can put one foot forward, the other must press back.

Crucially, nothing is ever completely *yin* or *yang*. A *yin* situation always contains the seeds of its *yang* complement, and vice versa. You can see that within the *taijitu* ☯. Those seeds are represented by the dot of black inside the white, and the dot of white inside the black. The aggressive person offers a real-life example: his *yang* explosiveness is evident, though it probably hides a seed of *yin* insecurity.

The Daoists see cyclicality as inevitable. *Yin* eventually transforms into *yang*, and vice versa. In this cyclicality, *yin* and *yang* 'arise mutually.' This mutual arising is a fundamental aspect of Chinese philosophy, termed *xiang sheng* (giving birth to each other).[5]

The Daoist classic *Daodejing* puts it this way in verse 2:

Being and non-being produce each other.
Difficult and easy complement each other.
Long and short define each other.
High and low oppose each other.
Fore and aft follow each other.

And in verse 58:

Good fortune has its roots in disaster,
and disaster lurks with good fortune.
Who knows why these things happen,
or when this cycle will end?
Good things seem to change into bad,
and bad things often turn out for good.
These things have always been hard to comprehend.

---

5   Appendix 3 is a brief glossary and guide to pronunciation.

When the *yang* in a situation is evident, the Daoist looks for where the *yin* is hiding and finds the relevance of the interplay, and vice versa.

By sensing the *yin* and *yang* in a situation, you can better discern the flows of energy, and see opportunities and threats. This can help you as a leader or in your life more generally. An opportunity frequently hides inside a threat, and vice versa. The stories in the following chapters illustrate this in practice.

However, these cycles are not the simple to-and-fro of a pendulum's swing. They form a dialectical process. That is, there is dialogue between *yin* and *yang*, which creates a new state and a further complementary opposite. These two new states, in turn, interact and the process continues, like a kaleidoscope. This view of the holistic and dynamic is characteristic of Daoism, and indeed of Asian philosophy more broadly.[6]

So, where can you try to observe *yin* and *yang*, and why should you pay attention to them? How can you become more adept at working with them?

**Your body.** You can start by noticing the *yin* and *yang* in your body. The whole of Traditional Chinese Medicine (TCM) is based on balancing *yin* and *yang*. TCM is beyond the scope of this book, but let's focus briefly on your nervous system.

Your sympathetic nervous system (the *yang* part) is activated by danger or stress. It gets you ready for 'flight, fight or freeze.' In contrast, your parasympathetic nervous system (the *yin* part) regulates your 'rest and digest' or 'feed and breed' functions. The problem with today's hectic pace is that it can nudge you deeply into the *yang* mode.

If you spend too much time in that *yang* state, you do not have time to nourish and heal your body. This leads to problems with sleep, muscle stiffness, feelings of frustration,

---

6   See Peng, "Naïve Dialecticism and the Tao of Chinese Thought."

and anxiety. You risk becoming locked into this mode. Too much continuous *yang* means your brain becomes hard-wired – literally. When you are calm, signals from your sensory organs first travel mainly to your neocortex. This is the 'rational' part of your brain, which decides whether to pass the signal on for action. If an external threat needs urgent action, your neocortex passes the signal to your amygdala. Deep in your brain, your amygdala then releases adrenaline and cortisol to prepare you for fight, flight or freeze. However, under relentless stress and anxiety, the wiring that runs from your sensory organs directly to your amygdala get upgraded to full-fibre broadband, while your rational neocortex remains on dial-up. Slight threats produce immediate and extreme reactions. In his book *Emotional Intelligence*, psychologist Daniel Goleman called this amygdala hijack … but you could also call it neocortex bypass.

In contrast, by balancing these two modes of *yin* and *yang* you can gain energy, health and calmness. Ask: Am I balancing these two modes? What changes in my work or social routines could benefit me?

**Your level of activity.** Many of us blast through the day expressing *yang* energy, only to slump down in a *yin* state of exhaustion at the end of the day. Perhaps this is OK. But perhaps you can spread out the *yang* and *yin* more evenly. You could even go as far as to take a nap midday, as Winston Churchill and Margaret Thatcher did. This can help you keep your internal battery charged, rather than frequently running it flat and thus eroding it.

**Your mood.** Most people experience periods of exuberance (*yang*) and periods of unhappiness (*yin*). If you remain attuned to both *yin* and *yang*, you can see the embers of happy *yang* in an unhappy *yin* situation. By perceiving this, you can then fan the embers of happy *yang* back to life. This can help you become more resilient.

Conversely, it's good to recognize in a happy *yang* period that *yin* will eventually pop up, and to be prepared for that. This is another source of resilience.

**Your relationship with your partner or close friends.** Are you someone who talks (*yang*) more than you listen (*yin*), or vice versa? If you talk a lot, doing more listening can help you learn, and encourage others to engage with you. If you are the listening type, then expressing yourself more can help you share your vision. This can inspire others and help you engage with their manifestation of the Dao.

**The team or organization you lead.** Effective leaders can sense the *yin* and *yang* in their teams. For example, they know which of their colleagues are more *yin* reflective types, and which are more *yang* doers. Great leaders know how to combine these energy sources for greater team power, as we will see.

## BENEFITS AND YOUR DEVELOPMENT

By attuning yourself more to the *yin* and *yang* in the world and in yourself, you can gain a deeper and wider view of what is going on. You will make wiser use of your energy, and recharge your energy levels more effectively; become more creative as an individual or team leader; and build better relationships as you master the dance of interaction with your conversation partner.

By attending merely to this first principle, your life starts to develop more flow. To gain these benefits, steps to understand *yin-yang* include:

1. **Practice sensing *yin* and *yang* in different situations.** For example, art and architecture have both positive structures and negative spaces. Music has loud and quiet; fast and slow; triumphant and sentimental. Rivers have

gushing torrents and limpid pools. Mood can be manic and depressive. Fine-tune your ability to notice *yin* and *yang*, and see how one might be hiding inside the other.

2. **Sensitize your antennae to how *yin* may change into *yang* and back again, and notice the energy flows.** You can sense these transitions even as you walk. You can start with a *yin* amble, stroll or saunter; then switch into a *yang* march, strut or swagger. Try some tai chi. Notice the ebbs and flows of conversations, team discussions or arguments.

3. **Experiment consciously, and perhaps radically, with trying more *yin* or more *yang*.** Notice what happens when you amp up your *yin* or *yang*. Play with being more *yin* (e.g. receptive) or *yang* (e.g. assertive) than you might otherwise be in a given situation.

## THE MAXIMS AND STORIES

In the following three chapters, *Brush Stops, Meaning Continues* explores the core aspects of *yin-yang* energy flows. *Pierce Wall, Steal Light* illustrates the oft-overlooked power of *yin*, and the cyclicality of *yin-yang*. *Eight Immortals Cross the Sea* shows how *yin-yang* diversity can contribute to a team's success.

As you read these stories, it is useful to ask yourself:

- Where are the *yin* and *yang* in the story?
- How can I discern *yin* and *yang* in my own life more deeply? How do they 'arise mutually'? What does that imply for me?
- How does – or could – managing the interplay between *yin* and *yang* create more energy for me?

After reading the stories, you might decide you want to further develop your insights into *yin-yang* energy flows. If so, use the template following each story to help you plan your growth.

# 意 到 筆 不 到

yi dao bi bu dao

# 1. BRUSH STOPS, MEANING CONTINUES

Embracing the power of *yin*
to achieve more through less

I prepare to paint.

Yesterday I had cleared the table of distracting objects. This morning I cleared my mind of distracting thoughts. Now I am ready. The four treasures of Chinese painting arranged in front of me: brush, ink-stone, ink-block and paper.

I start to paint a landscape in the Chinese style of ink wash. The first, lighter washes of distant mountains turn out well.

My pencil sketch of the landscape is propped up in front of me. I grind the ink-block against the stone and add a few drops of water. I smudge a few peaks to create some clouds. The shoulders of nearby hills emerge in the middle distance – from the serendipity of the ink's flow. Shorter, stabbing strokes create a forest and a solitary pine in the foreground, next to the stream. The hermit's hat emerges as an accidental masterpiece. Offshore a small flotilla of fishermen's boats emerges, unbidden. Tiny figures bend over the stern to pull in a fishing net. You can practically feel them straining.

The painting is perfect. I call my painting master and he comes to see it a few days later. "Not bad," he says, "... but the painting does not really work ..."

Crestfallen, I glance at him askance. He says nothing. I follow his roving gaze to discern where the painting might be falling short. I raise both eyebrows higher in inquiry.

He waits and waits. At last, the empty space in the conversation triggers in me an inkling of understanding.

"The brushstrokes are pretty good," I say, "... but I guess the picture is too full, too busy ... too much ink and not enough empty space. If I'd spared the brush, the painting might have had more meaning."

Cramming too much into a painting or conversation can be counter-productive.

---

In 1679, there appeared in China an influential painting manual. Filled with valuable maxims and archetypal images, the *Manual of the Mustard Seed Garden* presented tips and techniques drawn from the country's old masters. It inspired hundreds of painters over many centuries, in both China and Japan.

One of its maxims – 'Brush Stops, Meaning Continues' – is incredibly rich in insights. It is a Swiss Army knife that you can unfold to use in many situations, not just in painting.

The essence of that maxim is: even vacant space – apparently empty and void, where the brush has not arrived – can carry meaning. The space is, in fact, pregnant with potential power. Any masterpiece relies as much on the space between the brushstrokes as on the painted parts, because it relies on the interplay between them.

For the Daoist, this is a manifestation of *yin-yang* energy flows. Any painting needs a bit of driven, positive-principle *yang.* But it also needs some receptive, negative-principle *yin.* The tension between *yin* and *yang* creates energy, and energy creates power. Though the paintbrush has stopped, the meaning has not, and the meaning indeed has more power when the whole painting includes complementary empty space.

The maxim has further nuances. Any conversation needs both *yin* and *yang.* A conversation may have gaps, pauses and unsaid words, but those vacancies may indeed be laden with meaning. Our friend or colleague may not paint their thoughts and meanings out loud for us. Of course, that does not mean those thoughts do not exist – the person may just be unable or unwilling to express them. We may have writer's block, but that does not mean we lack things to say. You get the drift: any aspect of living needs both *yin* and *yang.*

You can see this in works of fiction too. Great novels often engage the reader because the author omits things, so the reader can fill them in. Umberto Eco carried this to an extreme. He was the father of the 'open text' school of fiction in which the author offers details only sparingly. Leaving stuff out can be powerful: it actively engages the 'existential credentials' of the interpreter as she or he provides the missing details.[7]

Paulo Coelho offers a further example. In *The Alchemist*, he often forsakes the details when talking of deserts, trees and even people. When he writes of crossing a desert, he leaves us, the readers, to fill in our preferred images of that desert. In doing so, we gain more from our interaction with the book.

---

7   Commenting on Eco's 'Open Text' and the poetics of openness, Cary Campbell of Simon Fraser University says that 'open text' engages by offering multiple interpretations.

William Goldman was a novelist, playwright and one of Hollywood's most successful screenwriters. He won Academy Awards for *Butch Cassidy and the Sundance Kid* and *All the President's Men*. When coaching aspiring writers on how to engage an audience, his first advice was, "Make 'em laugh, and make 'em cry …. but most importantly, make 'em wait!" The power of the pregnant pause emerges again …

In M. Night Shyamalan's 2004 movie *The Village*, our terror is sustained for most of the story by demons whose faces and actions we do not see. The elders refer continually to "those of whom we must not speak." Empty space has power.

These and other examples show clearly how the principle of *yin-yang* is embedded deep within the maxim 'Brush (or pen) stops, meaning continues.' When we fill a discussion or project with too much purposeful *yang*, we deny the power of receptive *yin* to contribute.

———————————

To help us understand how we can apply this maxim, let's first pause briefly to notice the first character of the phrase: 意, which stands for 'meaning.'

A simple translation from the Chinese would be: idea, meaning, thought. But the character carries other powerful nuance too: wish, desire, intention, to expect, to anticipate.

We gain a deeper understanding if we look at this character's etymology. Looking closely, you can see that 意 is built up from the character 音 *speech* at the top and 心 *mind* at the bottom. So, this first full character of the maxim implies 'speech of the mind.' And that character 心 for *mind*, with its central pump and peripheral signs of blood in flow, also signifies *heart* and *soul*, as we shall see later.

So, a deep literal reading of this chapter's maxim would be: the speech of the heart-mind-soul arrives, even though our utterance through brush, pen or spoken word does not.

———————————

There are at least three distinct ways to use this maxim.

First, it can remind us to **not overfill the pot**. Even experienced leaders and managers can talk too much, tempted to be over-generous with their advice. This can leave too little space in the conversation for the other person to express their own observations, feelings and motivations. See your contributions to the conversation as not just your *yang* statements, but also as the brushstrokes that define the empty *yin* spaces into which the other person can engage. Some of the best conversations may emerge when there are pauses that are uncomfortably long ...

In *Art and Illusion*, distinguished art historian Ernst Gombrich translates this maxim. His version is 'ideas present, brush may be spared performance.' For the charismatic leader, this means not painting a full and final vision of the future – but instead leaving spaces for others to fill in and thus commit to the vision. We all have a friend who gushes and talks all the time; it's not very attractive. As an artist, make sure that the canvas you paint or the photo you take has enough empty space. This creates a flow of energy between those spaces and the filled-in parts.

Secondly, the maxim reminds us to **discern the subtext in a situation**. The subtext is the hidden or less obvious meaning in a situation. Few people speak exactly what they are thinking, and even fewer express all their feelings. Screenwriting guru Robert McKee tells us in his brilliant book and masterclasses, entitled *Story*, that the surest way to have your film script rejected is to write 'on the nose.'

This Hollywood term refers to creating characters who always say exactly what they mean. But this is not faithful to real life. Subtext is omnipresent, which is why Hollywood requires it.

For example, Don Corleone in *The Godfather* does not explain in detail about how his adversary will suffer. He does not say that his adversary will wake up next to the severed head of his favourite, million-dollar racehorse. He merely whispers that he's gonna make him an offer he cannot refuse. The meaning arrives, though the screenwriter's brush has stopped.

In the flow of an everyday conversation, it is easy to overlook subtext, but this maxim can keep us alert to it.

Thirdly, the maxim can help you if **you have writer's block**, or feel some other impediment to expressing yourself. It can give you courage to progress your project even if you have not yet brought it to life in a tangible way.

This third application uses a slightly different reading of the maxim. The variant is: even though your brush or pen has stopped, your meaning does still exist, even if it's still only inside your head ... Times of fallow fields and wallowing feelings can indeed be pregnant with energy.

**RECAP**

*Brush Stops, Meaning Continues* is a maxim that reminds us to engage the power of *yin*. The power of positive *yang* is usually very evident. But a battery with only one terminal will never work. By noticing both *yin* and *yang*, and encouraging the subtle interplay between them, you can create more motivation in yourself and others. Recalling this maxim can prompt you to:

- **Engage more deeply with people** – by creating space for their contributions.
- **Be more aware of your surroundings** – by tuning in to the subtexts.
- **Persevere in your own creative acts** – by recognizing that the ideas are there, even if you are not yet sure how to express them.

# EXPLORING THE MAXIM

*[See the following page for a worked example]*

1. Reflect: What aspects of this maxim resonated most with me?

   .

   .

   .

   .

   .

   .

2. Consider: Where and how could this maxim help me, right now?

   .

   .

   .

   .

3. Plan (optional): Define a relevant goal and how to get there *

   GOAL: *specific goal related to focus area: measurable, achievable*

   .

   REALITY: *where I am on achieving this goal: evidence from present / past*

   .

   .

   OPTIONS: *3-4 different options to achieve my goal*

   .

   .

   WAY FORWARD: *Chosen option: first step, by when, support needed*

   .

   .

   .

*See Chapter 17 for a worked example of using this GROW method.

# EXPLORING THE MAXIM

**1.** Reflect: What aspects of this maxim resonated most with me?

- Liked the idea of using more 'yin,' not just 'yang' all the time — the power of empty space and receptivity
- Liked the idea of the way yin and yang influence each other and create something new — like mentioned in Chapter 1
- ...

**2.** Consider: Where and how could this maxim help me right now?

- I was recently promoted to manage a troubled restaurant site.
- I have been very directive — issuing instructions — for the last two weeks. Need to complement this 'telling' with more 'asking.'
- Looking at the yin-yang dynamics of the team could help me.
- ...
- 

**3.** Plan (optional): Define a relevant goal and how to get there *

GOAL: *specific goal related to focus area: measurable, achievable*
- Gain more commitment from staff, by applying yin-yang thinking at work every day for three weeks. Then do a staff satisfaction survey.

REALITY: *where I am on achieving this goal: evidence from present / past*
- I've told the staff my plans — I've been very clear / directive / 'yang'
- Directive is my normal way to manage teams
- Staff have complied but become quiet / surly; restaurant has less 'buzz'

OPTIONS: *3-4 different options to achieve my goal*
- Use yin: go on a 'listening tour' to get staff input and show I care about their views, OR ...
- Map out the yin-yang energy flows between the team members to help spot the issues, OR ...

WAY FORWARD: *Chosen option: first step, by when, support needed*
- Go on a 'listening tour' — ask each team member's views on how we should turn around the restaurant. Engage in a nonthreatening way.
- Write down my agenda for the conversations and how I will position the conversation.
- 

*See Chapter 17 for a worked example of using this GROW method.

# 鑿壁偷光

zao bi tou guang

# 2. PIERCE WALL, STEAL LIGHT

Using *yin-yang* thinking
to become more creative

Years ago, during the Western Han Dynasty (202 BCE–220 CE), there was a young man named Kuang Heng. His family was very poor, and he had to work hard in the fields all day, every day.

But Kuang wanted to go to school, just as the children of his wealthier neighbours did. He wanted to study, then take the civil service exams that would earn him a career serving the emperor. His friends laughed at his ambition. But whenever he could, Kuang hid outside the schoolroom and listened to the teacher's lessons through a crack in the school wall.

His family could not afford to send him to school, but a relative took pity on him and taught him how to read. In time ,Kuang realized that he could learn by himself.

To pass the exams, he would need to read all the great Chinese classics. He tried to borrow books so he could read them when he was not working in the fields. But only rich people had books. No one would risk lending them to a poor boy who might steal them. Kuang had an idea. He went to the biggest house in the village and convinced the owner to lend him books in exchange for his labours.

Kuang Heng worked the fields from dawn to dusk every day, but he managed to read short sections of the books while he ate lunch. He wanted to study at night too. But his family could not afford oil for the lamp. It was taking Kuang ten and a half months to read a single volume.

One night, when Kuang Heng got home, the surrounding area was pitch black except for the light streaming through the windows of a neighbour's house. Kuang smacked his head. "Why didn't I think of it before!"

When he got home, he checked the wall that he shared with his neighbour's house. He found a crack and gently made it a bit bigger. After a while, he made it big enough that a tiny ray of light shone through. Kuang Heng was excited but dared not dig further. There was just enough light for reading. Kuang finally passed the exams and became a scholar.

He had pierced the wall to steal the light.

———————

More than 50 generations of children in China have heard this story. It clearly promotes the values of education and perseverance.

Yet the story also illuminates two important lessons of *yin-yang* that are less frequently highlighted. Did you spot them?

Crucially, Kuang's solution rests on creating the *yin* hole in the wall. This is what let the *yang* light stream in. This idea also appears earlier, when he listens to the *yang* voice of the teacher through the *yin* crack in the school wall. The story illustrates with great clarity the potential and power that is latent within the apparent emptiness of *yin*. It shows how we can arrive at creative solutions by combining *yin* and *yang*.

This motif of the power of *yin* appears often in Daoism. For example, verse 11 of *Daodejing* reads:

> Thirty spokes are joined together in a wheel, but it is the centre hole that allows the wheel to function.
> We mould clay into a pot, but it is the emptiness inside that makes the vessel useful.
> We fashion wood for a house, but it is the emptiness inside that makes it liveable.
> We work with the substantial, but the emptiness is what we use.

This hints at a second aspect of *yin-yang* energy flows. It becomes evident only when we see the arc of Kuang Heng's later life.

Kuang was a real-life person and his career is well-recorded.[8] He tried the civil service exams nine times and finally graduated. His low grade did not qualify him as an official, but it did license him to write and lecture. He rose through the ranks based on his peerless understanding of the classic *Book of Songs*. Emperor Yuan eventually appointed him Prime Minister of the whole of China in 36 BCE.

Kuang received a title and land in the countryside. But he introduced a grain of negative *yin* into this positive *yang*-like situation. He exploited an inaccuracy in a county map to expand his fiefdom by 20 square kilometres. The error was discovered, but he used his prestige and power to have his accountant cook the books and cover up the details. The crime was eventually discovered. Kuang was found guilty

---

8    For example, in *The Book of Han* (*Hanshu*) 81.3346.

of stealing land, and more crucially of impiety. He was demoted to commoner and eventually died in poverty.

Here we see the second, dynamic aspect of *yin-yang* energy flows at work. In Kuang's career we see the cyclicality of rise and fall. Even from his childhood, we see in Kuang's *yang* determination a hint of the *yin* stealing. As noted earlier, every *yang* contains some *yin* – and vice versa. In this case, as the Kabballah says: the end is in the beginning and the beginning is in the end. Parenthetically, there is a poetic justice in the fact that Kuang's turning points in life were played out through books: the books of Kuang's initial studies, the *Book of Songs* that was the platform for his promotion, and the cooked books that caused his downfall.

---

Let's look at three specific ways in which working *with yin-yang* energy flows can help us, with this phrase 'pierce wall, steal light' as a reminder.

First, you can use *yin-yang* thinking to find **more creative solutions to a problem you face**. For example, as the leader of an organization or team, you have probably set up brainstorming sessions to solve problems. You may have used the Six Thinking Hats. These originated with Edward de Bono, in his book of the same name. This approach has each team member look at a given challenge from one of six perspectives. One person uses the Yellow Hat, and suggests solutions from the viewpoint of 'the optimist.' The Blue Hat is 'the conductor'; the Green Hat is 'the creative'; the Red Hat is 'the heart'; the Black Hat is 'the judge'; and the White Hat is 'the factual.'

But a simpler approach uses *yin-yang* hats to yield even greater creativity. Some team members first wear a *yang* hat and argue forcefully for a particular solution; the other team members wear a *yin* hat and argue against the idea. Crucially, you then ask the team to swap hats, so the proposers become the naysayers, and vice versa. This not only elicits all the *yin* and *yang* aspects of the situation, but also starts to build support for the final, emergent decision.

Another form of creativity uses a focus on the *yin*. For example, when confronted with obstacles and challenges, a natural temptation is to put more manpower, energy or money behind the *yang* idea to force a way forward. But you can often make easier and greater breakthroughs by using *yin* instead of *yang*.

Certain military strategies present a classic example of using *yin*. For example, they use a small team to disrupt the enemy's supply lines, rather than a vast force to battle the enemy head-on. The ultimate military example of using *yin* is the feigned retreat. This tactic involves appearing to run away from the enemy, luring them to follow. But then the enemy is pounced upon from unexpected quarters, and eventually routed. Sun Tzu advocates this in his well known *The Art of War*, dating from the 5th century BCE. Many other commanders have used this tactic, including the Spartans at the Battle of Thermopylae, and the Nazis at the Battle of Kasserine Pass in 1943. The *yin* of feigned retreat can beat the *yang* of advancing full-tilt.

Second, you can use *yin-yang* thinking **to help yourself or your team address apparently irreconcilable differences.**

Niels Bohr won the Nobel Prize for Physics in 1922, based on his groundbreaking contributions to quantum mechanics. His Nobel citation reads: "For his services in the investigation of the structure of atoms and of the radiation emanating from them."

Bohr succeeded in his research because he refused to accept the dogma of the 1920s. This stated that something was either a wave of energy or a particle. Bohr instead contended that something could be both a wave and a particle at the same time. It just sometimes looked more like one than the other. He saw wave and particle as interconvertible *yin* and *yang*, with a grain of each in the other.

In 1947, Bohr's native Denmark awarded him an honour normally reserved for royalty. He was allowed a coat-of-arms and chose to feature the *yin-yang* symbol *taijitu* ☯ on it prominently!

In daily life, this *yin-yang* mindset can help you with relationships. Few colleagues, friends or family members consistently live up to the image we may have created of them. Someone we think of as the 'happy' person contains an element of sadness. The 'creative' person sometime shows regimented habits. The 'energetic' person has periods of downtime. If we recognize that we all have both *yin* and *yang*, and that we can switch dynamically and sometimes unforeseeably between states, we may appreciate each other more, form more constructive relationships with others and potentially reconcile differences.

Finally, *yin-yang* awareness can **alert you to impending or potential changes in your surroundings.** Nowhere is this clearer than in the global physical environment. Here, climate disasters reveal a push-back against the *yang* ways in which mankind has used the planet's natural resources.

Everyday materials, too, offer an interesting illustration of the dynamics of *yin-yang* energy flows. Think about water. Here, a tiny change in temperature – just a fraction of a degree – can make a huge difference as ice turns to water, and water turns to steam. They are all still $H_2O$, but these states have very different properties. Physicists call these transitions 'phase changes.' When systems like societies, corporations and economies have complex structures, tiny changes in the environment can ripple through to create massive phase changes in the system. This idea has been called the Butterfly Effect, popularized in *The Simpsons*, *The Terminator*, *Back to the Future*, *X-Men*, *Jurassic Park*, etc. An imagined butterfly merely flapping its wings in South America could conceivably, through a string of small but linked events, change the weather in Texas from a *yang* sunny day to a *yin* hurricane.

In daily life, this suggests staying alert to how *yang* will inevitably flip to *yin* and vice versa.

---

**RECAP**

*Pierce Wall, Steal Light* is a maxim that reminds us of the power of *yin*, and also that *yin-yang* energy flows are dynamic. Recalling this maxim can prompt you to:

- **Solve problems in more creative ways** – as illustrated by the *yin-yang* hats exercise, and the philosophy underlying the *yin* feigned military retreat.
- **Unite apparent opposites** – as Niels Bohr did with his wave-particle model of light.
- **Alert you to forthcoming changes** – if you can see the grain of *yang* in a *yin* situation, and vice versa.

# EXPLORING THE MAXIM

1. Reflect: What aspects of this maxim resonated most with me?

    .
    .
    .
    .
    .
    .

2. Consider: Where and how could this maxim help me right now?

    .
    .
    .
    .
    .

3. Plan (optional): Define a relevant goal and how to get there *

    GOAL: *specific goal related to focus area: measurable, achievable*

    .

    REALITY: *where I am on achieving this goal: evidence from present / past*

    .
    .

    OPTIONS: *3-4 different options to achieve my goal*

    .
    .

    WAY FORWARD: *Chosen option: first step, by when, support needed*

    .
    .
    .

*See Chapter 17 for a worked example of using this GROW method.

NOTES

# 八 仙 過 海

ba xian guo hai

# 3. EIGHT IMMORTALS CROSS THE SEA

Combining *yin* and *yang* skills
to empower the team

The Eight Immortals inhabit a special place in the heart-minds of the Chinese, and the Daoist story of how they crossed the East Sea is a favourite throughout China. It is also a story with *yin-yang* elements relevant to us all.

The Immortals are legendary Daoists who achieved spiritual success through study, good works and inherent virtues. They became immortal god-like beings (*xian*). The character for *xian* '仙' combines the figure of a man on the left, and a mountain on the right. This is because the Immortals often reached enlightenment by meditating on remote mountain tops.

The Eight Immortals are loved for four main reasons. First, they had started as ordinary people, so they show that you can achieve phenomenal results if you work hard on selfcultivation. Second, they were drawn from all walks of life. They ranged from nobles to commoners – so everyone can identify with at least one character in the story. Third, they are accessible. They turn up, unbidden, to help the poor and needy. You do not need to pray to them or make sacrifices, as demanded by the gods of many religions! Finally, they each have a magic skill – just as we all feel we might have, on a good day ...

The story of how they crossed the sea developed over centuries. Our oldest source is from the book *The Journey to the East,* written around 1525.

---

One day the Eight Immortals were sitting and having a drink at Penglai Pavilion, as they often did.

First, there is iron-crutch Li. He had been a beggar; his magic object is a gourd bottle. From it he dispenses cures and help for the needy. Then there is Lu. He had been a scholar; his magic object is a pair of *yin-yang* swords. Han Zhongli was an army general; his magic object is a banana leaf fan. His cousin, Han Xiangzi, was a high official; his magic object is a flute. Fairy He is a prophet; her magic object is a lotus flower. Lan is a street-performer; his magic object is a wicker basket, and sometimes his musical clappers made of jade. Cao was an emperor; his magic object is a jade tablet. Zhang was a recluse; his magic object is a drum. He often faces backwards as he rides his mule. This symbolizes that to go forwards, we may need to defy conventions and change our habits.

A messenger approaches the group. He bears an invitation to the birthday party of the great Jade Emperor on nearby Penglai Island.

The Immortals accept. Lu is tipsy and says, "Instead of getting there by riding the clouds like we normally do, why don't we try something different? Let's go to the shoreline and use our magical objects to get across. Let's see who gets there first!"

The Immortals love the idea. Iron-crutch Li casts his crutch into the waves; it becomes a canoe and he paddles ahead. Han Xiangzi copies him with his flute and gives chase. Han Zhongli is next, turning his banana leaf fan into a surfboard. Lan gives chase, hopping across in his wicker basket. Zhang retrieves his magic donkey from his wallet, unfolds it (!), then rides over the waves. Lu skis across on his pair of his *yin-yang* swords. Then Cao jumps in and rides his jade tablet. Fairy He floats effortlessly over the waves on her lotus flower.

But their antics disturb the tyrant Dragon King of the East, who rules the region. He sends his shrimp soldiers and crab generals to investigate. Lan is lagging behind as his wicker basket takes on water. The shrimps and crabs spot him from the reflection off his musical clappers, and kidnap him. But the Dragon King wants *all* the magic objects, so he holds Lan hostage.

The Immortals notice that Lan is missing. "Perhaps he drowned," says Lu. "... he was a heavy drinker."

"Nonsense," replies Zhang. "He is one of us. It's your duty to search for him. It was your idea to cross the sea this way."

The Immortals eventually find their way to the Dragon King's palace, and demand Lan's release. A bloody battle ensues as the Dragon King summons reinforcements. Lu engages the Dragon King's son in mortal combat. But the son is no match for Lu's *yin-yang* swords. The tyrant's son senses defeat and turns to run, but his way is blocked by Fairy He. She eventually suffocates him with the scent from her lotus flower.

The action escalates as the Dragon King swears to avenge his son. He leads his 100,000 troops to kill the Eight Immortals. Han Zhongli, the former general turned Immortal, swipes his fan. He normally uses the fan to elevate the souls of the poor who died of starvation. But now he uses it to destroy half of the Dragon King's army. Meanwhile, Lu and iron-crutch Li release a deadly flame from Li's magic gourd. This incinerates their remaining enemies and even dries out the East Sea.

Victorious, the Immortals rest. But the Dragon King is still alive and has reinforcements. He persuades his uncles and cousins, who rule the other three oceans, to deluge the Immortals and drown them.

Luckily for the Immortals, Cao has his jade tablet. This has the power to part the seas, and the Immortals duly reach Penglai Island for the Jade Emperor's birthday party.

———————

It is the combinations of *yin* and *yang* that allowed the Immortals' team to triumph. The *yin* and *yang* in this story are less obvious than in the preceding chapter. Did you spot them?

Some of the Immortals are clearly more *yang* (Han Zhongli, the army general; Cao, the emperor). Others are more *yin* (Fairy He, the prophet; Lan, the street-performer). Interestingly, Lu, the scholar seems to represent both *yin* and *yang*. Indeed, he is armed with his dual *yin-yang* swords.

In addition, some of the magic objects are more *yang* (iron crutch; jade tablet), while others more *yin* (perfumed flower; arguably the banana leaf fan). But sometimes the *yin* object (flower) is used in a *yang* way (to suffocate the Dragon King's son).

During the battle, the Immortals use their combined *yin-yang* powers. And even at the end, when the Immortals seemed safe, Cao must use his *yang* jade tablet to create the *yin* parting of the East Sea. It is this combination of *yin-yang* that allows the Immortals to escape.

The story is an excellent demonstration of how big battles can be won if team members, each with special skills, act in concert. It suggests three questions, relevant for your daily life.

**First, what is my own particular magic gift**, and am I using it enough? This gift could be one you use pervasively, in many different settings – such as 'speed,' 'creativity,' 'storytelling' or 'understanding stakeholders.' I once worked with someone who had this latter gift. If you described a complicated programme of change required in a company, he could *instantly* see how to make it happen. Without hesitation, he could discern which stakeholders would be most affected. Instantly, he could list their concerns, how important those concerns would be, how to address those concerns, and in what sequence.

Alternatively, your magic gift could be a task-specific skill, like the carving skill of the cook we will meet in Chapter 13 (*Eye Not Whole Ox*). Or perhaps you are the barista who can make three cups of coffee at the same time, or the radiologist who always makes a correct diagnosis from the X-rays. Or perhaps your magic comes from having accumulated an encyclopaedic knowledge of a subject.

Very often, the magic formula is not a *single* skill or knowledge or trait – but rather a unique *combination* of such things. David Hockney, the famous painter, offers a vivid example. His success as an artist is global: in addition to his many honours and awards, in 2018 one of his paintings achieved the highest auction price of any living artist. His magic formula is not merely the *yang* of being able to apply paint to canvas. His magic formula is his ability to integrate his wide range of *yang* skills. He creates novel perspectives because he also uses his *yin* receptivity of observation, drawn from his wide range of experiences: as set designer, photographer, print-maker and digital savant. Hockney's magic formula is clearly multifaceted.

Of course, we all are all endowed with at least a hint of narcissism – so it's important to check the veracity for how magic our assumed formula really is!

**Second, what are the truly magical abilities of the people with whom I interact** – a person at work, in the family, a friend? Sure, some people seem 'good with people' or 'smart.' But have you ever stopped to pinpoint the specific ability that this person possesses? What is it that is truly distinctive? Is the person even aware of their gift? Knowing these things can help you give them appreciation, motivation and inspiration for how to deploy that gift.

For example, a colleague at work decided to leave her job because she felt she did not have the interest or skills to develop new clients or solve complex problems. She did not know what new job to seek. She became depressed. I had worked with her previously, and said that I thought her skills at interviewing people were remarkable. She initially dismissed this idea. How could you build a career on such a micro-level skill as interviewing? But we brainstormed it, and she thought that working in media might be attractive. Somehow, she rapidly landed an audition with a major TV network and went on to host her own programme … interviewing captains of industry on prime-time TV. Her undervalued *yin* skill of merely conducting research interviews became a *yang* skill of anchoring her own show.

Like the team of Eight Immortals, does your team have both *yin* and *yang* skills – some of which may be hidden?

**Third, as a leader, how can I create the conditions for the team to deploy their individual gifts in concert rather than in competition?** This can be hard to achieve. Even the Immortals show rivalry at the start of the story, as they compete to cross the sea. And even in the most purpose-driven teams, where the common goal is clear, team members are alert to how they are performing in comparison to their peers.

Leading a sales force offers a classic example. Productive salespeople are often motivated by achieving high personal sales. Sales force managers know this and often publish salesperson results in league tables to promote healthy rivalry. But managers then need a different approach if they are to encourage the salespeople to bring their individual talents to work together – for example, on an initiative of common good to the team or organization. (Things that can help are: repeatedly showcasing exemplary actions that achieved a common benefit; reinforcing this with visible rewards; nudging people into co—operation through pilot programmes that are exciting; and demonstrating the positive impact of collaboration – 'we built this brand *together*'; 'we *all* got a bigger bonus.') Thinking *yin-yang* can help.

Leading a family offers poignant examples of the challenge of creating the conditions for success, in which *yin* and *yang* characteristics can be combined. How do I gradually pinpoint the potential gift that each child has, and nurture it? How do I encourage teamwork: nudging Fred to teach Mary how to ride a bike, and Mary to help Fred with his algebra? How do I create the conditions for the unfolding family drama to be a comedy rather than a tragedy?

**RECAP**

The phrase *Eight Immortals Cross the Sea* reminds us to identify complementary *yin* and *yang* skills and combine them. Recalling this maxim can prompt you to:

- **Bring your own skills to bear more fully** – once you have identified your own unique magic formula of *yin* and *yang* skills.
- **Appreciate more fully the potential of colleagues, friends and family** – once you have considered the ways they can contribute to a common project.
- **Build collaboration within a team** – by creating the conditions for synergy between team members and their skills.

# EXPLORING THE MAXIM

1.  Reflect: What aspects of this maxim resonated most with me?

    .
    .
    .
    .
    .
    .

2.  Consider: Where and how could this maxim help me right now?

    .
    .
    .
    .
    .

3.  Plan (optional): Define a relevant goal and how to get there *

    GOAL: *specific goal related to focus area: measurable, achievable*

    .

    REALITY: *where I am on achieving this goal: evidence from present / past*

    .

    .

    OPTIONS: *3-4 different options to achieve my goal*

    .

    .

    .

    WAY FORWARD:  *Chosen option: first step, by when, support needed*

    .

    .

    .

*See Chapter 17 for a worked example of using this GROW method.

理
*li*

# PRINCIPLE 2

# *LI*

# (PATTERNS)

RECOGNIZE THE PATTERNS ...
TO SPOT WHEN AND HOW TO ACT

To make slate tiles from a block, you strike it sideways. You strike it along the planes of material laid down 500 million years ago. If you strike the block from any other direction, your potential tiles will shatter! Even greater care was required in ancient China when carving jade. Then, as now, this was a gemstone of incredible value. Ounce for ounce, it is still twice the price of gold. You could only shape this stone if you paid scrupulous attention to the faultlines created by the marbled veins.

*Li*, our second principle, means the underlying quintessential patterns of the cosmos – like the veins hidden in the jade block. They are also the patterns within your immediate environment or ecosystem. *Li* is also translated as 'principles,' 'reason,' 'order' and 'coherence.' Examples include the tangible patterns of our natural world; the physicist's Laws of Motion; and the underlying effects of supply and demand in economics. However we might struggle against them, those patterns and principles will eventually prevail.

Noticing and following the patterns can help you decide when and how to act in specific circumstances.

Slate and jade have patterns that are easy to spot. But the Daoist is also adept at seeing other patterns that are more subtle. This allows the Daoist to do things effortlessly, as we shall see. If you can notice and understand these patterns, you can accomplish more and with less effort. You can work with the grain when convenient to do so, rather than against it.

*Li* can also be translated as 'inherent pattern' or 'natural guidelines.' They are pointers to how your world works. Because of their crucial importance, the Daoists sometimes called these patterns *tian li* – Heavenly Patterns. In a similar vein, the science of physics is called *wuli* in Chinese – the *li* of things.

The Chinese character for *li* is 理. It combines jade (王) and interior (里) – originally representing those marbled veins within jade. (If you are interested in Chinese characters: the supremely precious jade, when written as a single character is 玉. This in turn represents something belonging to a 王 or king. And to go a level deeper still, the character for king '王' contains the traditional symbol for Heaven (the line at the top), Earth (at the bottom), and Humanity (in the middle) 三. The vertical line indicates the unifying role that the king was required to play.)

But which *li* patterns are most important to us? As we will see in Chapter 7 (*Go with Unfolding Nature*), the most obvious examples are in the physical world. The *li* here are the planes of the slate, the grain of the wood and the striation of the meat you are cutting. More complex patterns involve movement: do you hike over the hill or walk around it? (It turns out that animals, including we humans, have an uncanny knack for recognizing which terrain favours over-the-top and which favours skirting-around-the-edge.)

*Li* patterns clearly exist in time too – not just in space. The Daoist likes to sense the rhythms of their environment, because the patterns can signal a good time to act. They can also signal a good time to wait, as illustrated in Chapter 9 (*Calculated Waiting*). Some rhythms are obvious (if you take the time to sense them) – like that of your breathing and heartbeat. Indeed, one version of meditation works by aligning your breathing with your pulse rate. This helps you relax. It can also help you become more mindful, probably by tuning and toning your vagus nerve.[9]

*Li* patterns also exist in the way we interact with each other – within a specific relationship, or in a team, or across society. The ability to 'connect the dots' and recognize these patterns is a key skill for leaders, entrepreneurs, and for us all.[10] Patterns you have chosen to see as relevant might include things like: 'decisions made under extreme stress are typically not good ones.' Other examples include 'much of a person's reactions can be accounted for by their childhood experiences'; or 'Jim prefers to stick to the agenda, but Jane prefers to ski off-piste.'

As Salvador Dali said, "Knowing how to look is a way of inventing." Michelangelo famously had a similar view, that the sculpture was already complete within the marble block, before he started his work. It was already there; he just had to chisel away the superfluous material.

As the *Zhuangzi*, in Chapter 1 of that Daoist classic observes, we may, however, be oblivious to these patterns:

> The blind do not see the beauty of elegant figures,
> nor the deaf the sound of bells and drums.
> But is it only the bodily senses that experience deafness and blindness?
> There can also be a similar defect in the intelligence.

9   See, for example, Gerritsen, "Breath of Life: The Respiratory Vagal Stimulation Model."

10  Baron, "Opportunity Recognition as Pattern Recognition."

In other words (as we will see in Principle 4), while we do well to keep our antennae attuned for patterns and principles, we need to avoid becoming so wedded to a particular view of the cosmos that we blind our intelligence.

Philosophy professor Steve Coutinho, in *An Introduction to Daoist Philosophies*, relates patterns to the idea of channels of connection:

> In the *Zhuangzi* and *Liezi*, the natural patterns of things are understood through the metaphor of open channels: natural tendencies become possible directions of movement. These are conceived of metaphorically as a thinness, an emptiness – insubstantial channels that we are able somehow to become intuitively familiar with as we refine our own sensitivities.

Our ability to recognize patterns is perhaps the most important of our cognitive skills. In ancient hunter-gatherer societies, basic survival rested on recognizing patterns: 'looks like winter is coming – we'd better store food'; 's/he has symmetrical features and a strong body – would be an ideal mate.' As agricultural societies developed, more complex patterns had to be recognized: 'this land is moist but not swampy, and it is sheltered from the wind – let's plant here.'

The Industrial Age and the birth of modern science saw pattern recognition applied more broadly: 'burning coal can heat water; hot water creates steam; the pressure of the steam can power machinery; etc.'

Contemporary research highlights the crucial value of spotting and following underlying patterns. Neuroscientists argue that superior pattern processing is the essence of the evolved human brain.[11] As W. Brian Arthur, a leading economist from the distinguished Santa Fe Institute says,

"Research on cognition shows that our minds rarely make strictly logical deductions. Instead we rely on patterns – and on feelings associated with those patterns."[12] The value of pattern recognition in our commercial world is also clear. In *Profit Patterns*, authors Slywotzky et al. argue that: "The art of identifying, understanding and exploiting patterns needs to become part of the mental process of every decisionmaker interested in creating sustained profit growth."

But the Daoist's goal is not to create elegant scientific theories. The goal, instead, is to spot the underlying patterns, and then to engage with them in a practical way. As the classic *Zhuangzi* says of the sage, in section 15.2:

> In his stillness his virtue is the same as that of the Yin, and in movement his diffusiveness is like that of the Yang. He does not take the initiative in producing either happiness or calamity. He responds to the influence acting on him, and moves as he feels the pressure. He rises to act only when he is obliged to do so. He discards wisdom and the memories of the past; he follows the lines of Heaven-given nature; and therefore he suffers no calamity from Heaven, no involvement from things, no blame from men, and no reproof from the spirits of the dead.

Keep it simple; don't try to be too smart.

So, in what domains might *li* (patterns and principles) be most relevant for you, and how can you become more adept at working with them?

**The static physical world.** Patterns in nature – like those in slate – are the easiest to spot. The way that slate

---

11  Mattson, "Superior Pattern Processing Is the Essence of the Evolved Human Brain."

12  Arthur, "Decisions, Decisions."

splits proves that there really can be a 'right' (easy) way to solve a problem, if you look at it from the right point of view. There is also a 'wrong' way to address a problem if you fail to spot the pattern and approach it from the wrong angle.

To limber up and practice the pattern recognition that you can then apply in more complex situations, you can find and follow these patterns of nature. The whole field of biomimicry, mentioned in Chapter 17 (*Carp Leaps Dragon Gate*), uses nature's patterns to create useful materials such as Velcro.

**The dynamic physical world.** Patterns and principles in nature clearly exist not only in space but also in time. These rhythms may be regular or semi-regular. Obvious regular examples include the lapping of waves on the seashore and the swaying of a rope bridge in the wind. Even the way you walk has a rhythm. It is so unique to an individual that it can be used as evidence of identity in a court of law. Principle 5 (*Effortless Action*) includes a description of the rhythms of walking across mountains with minimal effort.

A whole branch of science is devoted to more complex dynamic patterns. Read up on chaos theory and catastrophe theory if you are interested. This discipline explores systems that appear to be chaotic, but in fact may have underlying rhythms.

Being able to recognize patterns in dynamic situations can help you time your initiatives to better effect. By knowing the dynamic patterns of attention, for example, you can better time the cadence of your speech as a presenter, or your punchline as a raconteur.

**Daily life.** In the business world, marketing (and specifically market segmentation) are areas where pattern recognition is crucial. Imagine you have written a book on, say, gardening. You are about to market it, and need to figure out how to price the book and how to promote it. To do that, you would need to know what 'segments' there are in the market. Some purchasers may be avid hobbyists. That could be one segment. Other purchasers might be armchair gardeners, others might be schools of gardening for which your book might become a standard text, and so on. Some of these segments will be bigger than others and warrant more marketing resources. Some will be willing to pay a higher or lower price. By understanding the *li* patterns and principles of these segments, you can make your marketing investments of effort and money to better effect. *Li* patterns and principles are important in many further arenas, some of which are illustrated in the stories in the next three chapters.

## BENEFITS AND YOUR DEVELOPMENT

By developing your ability to recognize the *li* patterns and principles of the cosmos, you increase your chances of finding extraordinary results with relative ease. You can create more innovative solutions, connecting the dots that you or others may previously have overlooked. (As Steve Jobs famously asserted, creativity is just connecting things.) You make better decisions, taking into account patterns in the subtly shifting dynamics of your environment and develop greater resilience, by grounding yourself in the fundamental principles of your environment, rather than in ephemeral fads.

To gain the benefits:

1. **Take time to notice patterns and principles.** That might sound obvious, but we run on autopilot for much of the time. When we do register some kind of pattern, we often do so subconsciously. Note what types of patterns are most valuable and intriguing for you: patterns in the world of people and psychology, or physics and the natural world, or in business?

Then deepen your grasp of how we recognize and use patterns. You can, of course, survive without that knowledge. But if you want to be an expert recognizer of patterns, it makes sense to know about the 'patterns of pattern recognition.' Current theories suggest that we use techniques such as template-matching, proto-type-matching and feature-analysis. More recent theories build on the success of information technology in the fields of neural networks, including convolution networks and recurrent networks.[13]

2. **Become T-shaped.** Excellent pattern recognizers tend to be T-shaped. They have a depth of experience in patterns in their main subject area (the vertical part of the 'T'). But they also have breadth across many other areas too (the cross-bar of the 'T'). Being a polymath allows you to spot patterns that others may have missed, by seeing analogies and applying metaphors.

3. **Accumulate a knowledge bank of relevant patterns and principles.** A memory of past patterns is crucial for being able to recognize new ones. London's cabbies offer a well-known example of this. They know the patterns and principles to apply when driving between any two places in London, under varying traffic conditions. The longer they spend as a taxi driver, the larger their posterior hippocampus becomes (the part of the brain associated with long-term memory).[14] Keep track of the patterns and principles in areas in which you want to develop insight.

---

13 Baron, "Opportunity Recognition: A Cognitive Perspective."

14 Maguire, "Navigation-related Structural Change in the Hippocampi of Taxi Drivers."

# THE MAXIMS AND STORIES

The following three chapters explore these themes in detail. *Crouching Tiger, Hidden Dragon* illustrates the core aspects of *li* patterns and principles. *Old Frontiersman Loses Horse* shows how a pattern can exist dynamically, across time. *Right Time, Right Place, People in Harmony* shows how patterns can include a wide range of factors – only some of which are controllable.

As you read these stories, it is useful to ask yourself:

- Which patterns and principles are most important to me – in life, at work and in relationships?
- Which patterns do I see most easily? Which might I typically overlook?
- Since pattern recognition is an important skill in all walks of life, how can I improve my ability to do it?

After reading the stories, you might decide to develop some aspect of your own *li* pattern recognition skills. If so, use the template following each story to help you plan your development.

# 臥 虎 藏 龍

wo hu cang long

# 4. CROUCHING TIGER, HIDDEN DRAGON

Uncovering hidden strengths
to live life more fully

"My dear Yu Xin, take care if you're going to hike up Mount Li," my host had warned a few hours earlier. "Lots of craggy rocks, fallen trees and rivers in spate. It's not like that fancy office of yours, back at the Imperial Palace in Xian. And if you don't come back, Emperor Wu will assume you've tried to escape back to the south. He'll send the army to get you! And watch out for Li himself – that black dragon has been prowling around lately ..."

I'm making good progress. The path underfoot is well trampled by others who have hiked up to see the pool that had emerged miraculously ten years ago. As I emerge from a forest and onto the shoulder of a ridge, I gain a commanding view. How much better to be up here than down in the flat and featureless plain surrounding my place of exile: the capital, Xian.

I try to clear my mind, but the intrigues back at the palace court swirl up in my mind. The eunuchs, who suddenly appear from behind silk curtains, crouching obsequiously but ready to stab you in the back. They had already murdered several emperors ... Then there's the Treasurer. He'd just persuaded the emperor to outlaw Buddhism. That had not even been for religious reasons, but just so the court could swell its coffers by selling the Buddhist palaces and gold ornaments, and by forcing the monks into productive labour so it could then be taxed. Things are never quite as they appear to be ...

On the other hand, my poems are selling well. They are read and recited in high places. Critics even talk of me as being the father of a glorious new era of Chinese poetry. I'm held here in the north against my will, but by injecting some southern rhythms into the poetry of the uncultured north, I have created something revered. Things are never quite as they appear to be ...

I pass the chrysanthemums that are fluttering in the breeze. I pause to prod around in search of the famous *lingzhi* mushrooms that reputedly grow up here, and unearth a few. Continuing, I reach a dark rock. It seems to be emitting a strange hiss. I stop. It's far too early in the season for the tigers to come down from the peaks, but you never know. Could a tiger be crouching behind that slab? I wait and then realize the hissing sound is too continuous – it must be the gushing of the nearby mountain stream. The patterns of nature are never quite as they appear to be ...

Relieved, I bound on ahead – only to fall flat on my face as I trip over a tree root. I glance down at it. It looks like the gnarled curling leg of a dragon. Must use that in my next poem. I make a mental note: 'crouching tiger, hidden dragon.'

——————

The Yu Xin of this story was a famous Chinese poet, who died in 552. He wrote a poem to the effect that 'the dark stone looks like a tiger is crouched behind it. The tree root looks like it conceals a dragon.' Fifteen hundred years later, Yu Xin's powerful phrase 'crouching tiger, hidden dragon' lives on in Chinese dialogue. And it lives on, of course, in the title of the movie that grossed over $200 million, won four Oscars, and received a further six Oscar nominations. Yu Xin remains an icon of Chinese poetry.[15]

The phrase is regularly said to symbolize 'hidden talents.' This is because, in China, the tiger and the dragon are both icons of powerful abilities. The tiger has long inspired both admiration and awe. It has prowess, ferocity and beauty. Its striped coat also suggests the creative interplay of complementary *yin-yang* energy flows. The tiger symbolizes the drive to achieve and develop. It is also a powerful protective motif, as its character 'hu' sounds the same as 護, meaning 'protect.'

What of the hidden dragon? The dragon is the most important of China's animal motifs. It pervades many aspects of Chinese culture. It is the mightiest of creatures, and since it frequently inhabits the clouds, it has power over the rain needed to sustain crops. The dragon is usually good-natured. Only the emperor was entitled to adopt its symbolic motif.

As metaphors, similes and allusions, these animals can help us think about ourselves and our own relationships. Chinese literature is not alone in recruiting their help. Examples abound, of course, in children's books, such as *Alice's Adventures in Wonderland*, *Winnie the Pooh* and *The Jungle Book*. But animals feature as protagonists in adult stories too: from *Aesop's Fables*, to *Beowulf*, to *Animal Farm*, to *The Hobbit*! In many other works they play walk-on but important parts too. Dante's *Divina Commedia*, for example, has the leopard, lion and she-wolf representing envy, pride and avarice, respectively.

---

15  Fuller, "An Introduction to Chinese Poetry."

'Crouching Tiger, Hidden Dragon' reminds us to spot a specific type of *li* pattern: patterns that relate to hidden talent. The phrase has many nuances that can help us in daily life, especially as a coach and leader.

If we follow the metaphor, we see that there are places – both visible, but also in our subconscious and in the unspoken subtexts of situations – where talents and other things of value may exist. These talents may be under-recognized, under-appreciated or under-used. Indeed, the Chinese character 藏 (*cang*) in the crouching tiger phrase means not just 'hidden, to conceal, to hide away' but also 'to harbour; to store' as well. The two sprigs of grass at the top of the character suggest a granary that stores nourishing grain. The character points not only to a veil of concealment, but also to the potential energy behind the veil.

Let's look at three specific ways this phrase can serve us in spotting the *li* – patterns and principles – as they relate to talent.

First, the maxim can **remind us to stay alert to overlooked talents and assets**. One of the roles of a leader is to be a breeder of other leaders in the team or organization. It's easy enough to rely on well-honed HR processes that try to create a conveyor belt of leaders. The lucky talents are spotted early in their lives. They quickly win glittering prizes. These prizes attract further recognition, in an easy upward soaring of success.

Others do not have it so easy, and their talent remains hidden until a friend or stranger intervenes. Who would have thought that a young black girl living on the breadline in the segregated deep south of the US, who suffered sexual abuse and had an unplanned teenage pregnancy, would have her talents recognized and become a successful philanthropist and businesswoman worth more than \$3 billion called Oprah Winfrey? Or that a boy whose parents were students, and who was returned by his first adoptive parents, would become Steve Jobs?

Perhaps the most enduring legacy we can create as a coach, leader or human being is to help another potential Oprah or Steve Jobs. If we can notice the hidden talent and turn on the switch or spotlight, we have done the world a service.

Second, the phrase can **prompt us to look for relevant storehouses of talent or skill**. These are places that may be replete with opportunity. A professional services firm that had largely relied on hiring MBAs from top US business schools noticed that the few accountants it had hired were doing remarkably well. The recruiting leaders explored that potential source of talent, and from that overlooked storehouse would eventually find many of its subsequent leaders.

Jack Welch, when leading GE, installed a discipline in which every division would rate itself, and other divisions, on a list of metrics such as customer service and profitability. Then, for each metric, the top-performing division shows the lowest performers how to improve. He found a way to discover and utilize the storehouses of skill within GE.

On a personal level, where are the storehouses of the people that can help us, but whom we have overlooked? If you are over 45 years old, the answer is almost certainly your 'advocates.' Your advocates are not people in your general network of contacts; they are people who have worked with you or seen you in action. If you are looking for a new job or role, your advocates are just about the only route to a new role. If you are in this age bracket, you probably think you only have 5-10 true advocates. But here's the rub – you probably have 100! Research by the Sloan School of

Management at MIT shows that recency of contact is irrelevant. An advocate with whom you have not talked with for ten years can be even more helpful than a more recent advocate.[16] Once an advocate, always an advocate. Advocates from the past often constitute a storehouse of hidden dragons ...

Third, it suggests that we **look for our own *inner* tigers and dragons**. What are the skills, talents, passions and sources of energy that you have decided to keep under wraps or under-nurtured? It might seem strange in an age of LinkedIn and self-promotion, but most people have skills and abilities that they are reluctant to promote.

As a child I cheekily asked my very able mother – with her PhD in botany and international renown as a historian of medieval gardens – why she did not promote herself more. She replied that if she put herself out there she might fail, and that would be embarrassing. I would later learn that in most of us lurks some fear of failure that causes us to keep some of our best lights hidden under a bushel.

Joseph Campbell was a world expert on the power of myth. Among his many claims to fame, he helped George Lucas knock the *Star Wars* storyline into best-selling form. In his book *The Hero with a Thousand Faces*, he dramatically portrays what happens when we refuse the call to use our unproclaimed abilities, and stick with the status quo instead:

"Refusal of the summons converts the adventure into its negative. Walled in boredom, hard work or 'culture,' the subject loses the power of significant affirmative action and becomes a victim to be saved. His flowering world becomes a wasteland of dry stones and his life feels meaningless – even though, like King Minos, he may through titanic effort

---

16  Levin, "The Power of Reconnection – How Dormant Ties Can Surprise You."

succeed in building an empire of renown. Whatever house he builds, it will be a house of death: a labyrinth of cyclopean walls to hide from him his minotaur. All he can do is create new problems for himself and await the gradual approach of his disintegration."[17]

Maybe the greatest value of Yu Xin's phrase is to nudge us into admitting, nurturing and exposing our inner crouching tigers and hidden dragons.

---

**RECAP**

*Crouching Tiger, Hidden Dragon* reminds us to keep a watchful eye on *li* patterns that can reveal hidden or overlooked opportunities in daily life and at work. A leader is a *li*-der! Recalling this maxim can prompt you to:

- **Build a stronger team** – by looking out for hidden talents.
- **Access best practices** – by finding places ('storehouses') of expertise that you can tap into.
- **Realize more of your own potential** – by examining your own inner tigers and dragons.

---

17  Campbell, *The Hero with a Thousand Faces*, p 49. Copyright © Joseph Campbell Foundation (jcf.org) 2008. Used with permission.

# EXPLORING THE MAXIM

1. Reflect: What aspects of this maxim resonated most with me?

    - .
    - .
    - .
    - .
    - .
    - .

2. Consider: Where and how could this maxim help me right now?

    - .
    - .
    - .
    - .
    - .

3. Plan (optional): Define a relevant goal and how to get there *

    GOAL: *specific goal related to focus area: measurable, achievable*

    - .

    REALITY: *where I am on achieving this goal: evidence from present / past*

    - .
    - .
    - .

    OPTIONS: *3-4 different options to achieve my goal*

    - .
    - .
    - .

    WAY FORWARD: *Chosen option: first step, by when, support needed*

    - .
    - .
    - .

*See Chapter 17 for a worked example of using this GROW method.

# 塞翁失馬

sai weng shi ma

# 5. OLD FRONTIERSMAN LOSES HORSE

Welcoming patterns of change
to improve resilience

Once upon a time there was a farmer called Sai Weng. He lived with his son in a tiny village in the remote northern region of China, close to the border. Life was hard, as the rains were unpredictable, and the vicious Xiongnu tribes continually threatened to sweep south across the border to loot and pillage.

Sai Weng loved his horse. He had reared it from when it was a foal. Now it was his transport and his powerful teammate. It was his only way to turn the huge pump that watered his crops.

One day, the horse ran away, or perhaps it just got lost. His neighbours commiserated with him. "Sai Weng! What a catastrophe! What a disaster!" they cried.

But Sai Weng was a Daoist. "Who knows whether it won't bring good luck?" he said. His neighbours thought he was mad.

A few days later, however, Sai Weng's horse returned. It brought a group of fine horses, raised by the barbarians of the steppe. "That's wonderful!" cried his neighbours. "You are the only household with so many horses!"

"Yes," said Sai Weng, "but who knows whether it will turn out to bring bad luck." His neighbours rolled their eyes. Surely this was a good thing?

Sai Weng's son loved to ride, and the next day tried to mount one of the new horses. But it had a wild streak and his son fell off and broke his thigh bone. Clearly a bad thing? "Maybe a good thing," observed Sai Weng.

"Awe c'mon," said his neighbours. "Now your son can't work the fields. We feel so sorry for you."

The barbarians invaded a year later. The army arrived to repel them and recruited all villagers of fighting age. The men strung their bows and went to battle. Nine out of ten villagers were killed. But some lived on. Sai Weng and his son both survived: the army had rejected Sai Weng's son because his old thigh injury had given him a permanent limp, and he successfully hid himself and his father from the Xiongnu.

———

This story is from the *Huainanzi*, an ancient Chinese collection of essays of mainly Daoist thought blended with a bit of Confucianism.[18] It was written sometime before 139 BCE. The essays emphasize the universal presence of *yin* and *yang*, and the *li* pattern of cyclical interplay between them. This theme is evident in the introduction to the original text of the 'frontier' story, which reads: "Bad luck brings good luck, and good luck brings bad luck. Misfortune and blessing turn into each other. It's a cycle, and you just can't tell what will happen next."

---

18  *Huainanzi*, section 18.5, accessed at https://ctext.org/huainanzi/ren-xian-xun [Author's translation].

The phrase 'Old Frontiersman Loses Horse' and its backstory are still told widely across China, Japan, Korea and Vietnam. There are Western expressions that are similar in meaning. But this Chinese version feels far more vivid, more dynamic and more complete – and therefore truer to real life.

English has expressions such as 'a blessing in disguise,' and 'every cloud has a silver lining,' for example. But each gets the job only half done, and the imagery feels remote; too abstract. The Islamic Sufis have a fable in a similar vein, in which the king asks the sages to create something that will make him happy when he is sad. The winner of this contest is a wise man who creates a ring inscribed with the reminder 'This too shall pass.' The ring works, and when the king is sad, he sees the ring and realizes that better days will come. The ring also works in reverse, and when the king is happy, he realizes that this too will pass. He becomes psychologically prepared for the next twist of fate.

The Chinese story and phrase work best for me, however. They show a plausible and tangible chain of events in a realistic way. They show the lively interplay between good luck and bad – rather than merely presenting us with a static cloud and its silver lining.

---

So, this is a story about a dynamic *li* pattern of change. In many *li* patterns and principles, you can identify aspects of positive *yang* and negative *yin*, and these are evident in this story. But the story goes beyond merely *yin* and *yang* to show a pattern across time, and Sai Weng's Daoist acceptance of it.

If we can see these types of patterns, we become more stable and have great resilience. This allows us to recognize life in the dialectical manner mentioned in the Introduction.

The maxim of this chapter offers us at least three lessons. All three are linked to an idea that we explored earlier: the *yin-yang* cycle of energy flows, and the *taijitu* ☯ explained earlier. This is that inside everything is a grain of its polar and complementary opposite. Everything dark contains a bit of lightness, and vice versa. Everything feminine contains a bit of masculine, and vice versa. This creates a *li* pattern in time. Every misfortune contains the potential for a blessing and vice versa. That grain of potential can grow, and flip a situation into its opposite.

Ideally, we should keep our minds open to seeing all this potential, in all these places. We should be alert to the possibilities and move instantly and effortlessly to engage with them. Just like the kung-fu master.

But there is a problem: our brains like to simplify things. It saves us mental energy if we can classify something, or someone, once and for all as positive or negative, good or bad, and not have to keep reevaluating. Most of us would have a hard time keeping an open mind about everything.

Thus the deeper message of this story cautions us not to lock on too quickly to conclusions about apparent situations. We should find a productive balance between certainty and open-mindedness. As Einstein said (in a slightly wordier version), "Everything should be made as simple as possible – but no simpler."[19] How can we best appreciate these patterns?

First, **stand far enough back from the situation that you can see the broader, evolving pattern.** Life is not a movie with a planned ending; it is a lengthy soap opera for which most of the script has not yet been written. The present scene is merely one frame in the show.

---

19  Robinson, "Did Einstein really say that?"

Whether we meet good or evil, we must look beyond the immediate time and space to take into account the extreme changes that may yet come. If we develop this habit – when blessings turn into misfortunes, or misfortunes turn into blessings – we develop our psychological resilience and endurance.

Second, **stay mentally nimble by avoiding labelling.** If we label our recent performance – whether at football, singing or having a difficult conversation – as a complete failure, we are less likely to learn from it. If we label someone else's performance as a failure, we are unlikely to learn from that too. If we go a step further and conclude that someone is bad or good, we have shelved our consideration of them and denied ourselves further observations and insights. If we label ourselves a hero, we become blind to how we can develop.

Conscious or unconscious labelling is an attempt to deny the unfolding continuation of a pattern across time. It is an attempt to freeze the grain of *yin* so that its negativity does not expand, or to ever-rely on the *yang*, hoping it will never wane.

Romantic relationships offer a powerful example of labelling. Especially in the early stages of courtship, there is a huge incentive to idealize: Yes! This person completes my life. Yes! This person gives me purpose. Yes! This person solves my loneliness. Quickly we lock in the idealized attributes of our would-be partner by attaching labels that are more positive than an independent observer would assign. Love indeed becomes blind.

The Daoists were adamant that labels and mental filters were normally a bad thing. We return to this in Principle 4 (*Simplicity*), where we examine the principle of *pu* simplicity.

**RECAP**

*Old Frontiersman Loses Horse* reminds us to stay aware of dynamic *li* patterns – not merely static ones. This enables you to:

- **See the bigger picture** – by taking a long-term view.
- **Stay mentally nimble** – by not attaching immutable labels to people or circumstances.
- **Be encouraged and resilient** – by recognizing that situations will prove to be neither entirely fortunate, nor entirely unfortunate.

# EXPLORING THE MAXIM

1. Reflect: What aspects of this maxim resonated most with me?

.
.
.
.
.
.

2. Consider: Where and how could this maxim help me right now?

.
.
.
.
.

3. Plan (optional): Define a relevant goal and how to get there *

GOAL: *specific goal related to focus area: measurable, achievable*
.

REALITY: *where I am on achieving this goal: evidence from present / past*
.

.

OPTIONS: *3-4 different options to achieve my goal*
.

.

WAY FORWARD: *Chosen option: first step, by when, support needed*
.

.

.

*See Chapter 17 for a worked example of using this GROW method.

# 天时 地利 人和

tian shi  di li  ren he

# 6. RIGHT TIME, RIGHT PEOPLE, RIGHT PLACE

Weighing three factors
to set up for success

Jim eased himself back from the vast mahogany table and went over to the windows that stretched from floor to ceiling in the meeting room on the top floor of United Industries' HQ building.

For a few minutes he gazed out over Manhattan's lesser skyscrapers, then went back to glance at the agenda for his imminent meeting. As CEO of the company, he was contemplating a $50 billion acquisition of a technology company in Germany. He had made many acquisitions in his career. But this one would be his biggest bet yet. He exchanged a few words with his chief financial officer and his human resources director – his immediate team for this venture.

The investment bankers arrived on time, in newly pressed suits, newly starched shirts and newly trimmed hair. They looked on top of their game. They looked like the Masters of the Universe that they claimed to be.

The bankers started their presentation by describing the general economic conditions. The economy in Europe was poised for recovery. Demand was starting to pick up. Business confidence was growing. Companies in Europe were generally undervalued. The conditions were auspicious for making an acquisition.

The bankers moved on to explain the strategic logic for making this particular purchase. Their presentation was comprehensive. Each product area was analysed in detail. For most products, the outlook for customers and competition were positive. There were many synergies and cost-savings available, and the target company was a good fit with United Industries' other businesses. This target company would be a great buy!

The bankers finished their presentation with a concise summary. Did Jim and his team have any questions? Everyone looked over to Jim.

"What are we missing?" asked Jim after a lengthy pause.

Everyone racked their brains. Jim was a wily fox. He must have something specific in mind.

"How about the people side of things?" asked Jim at last.

The bankers could not read Jim's mind and asked him to explain.

"Well, I know you guys focus on the financials and desk research. But you must have talked with some of the employees, or recent leavers or suppliers. What's the culture of the company? Will it fit with our culture? Is the top team cohesive? Are they any good? You know: that kind of thing."

"Of course, we would look into that, in the next stage of review," said the lead banker. "We normally consider that a secondary factor."

"Hmm," replied Jim as he slid a document across the mahogany table. "I was just reading this. It's by Oliver Engert. He's a senior partner at McKinsey. He quotes research suggesting that lack of cultural fit is the reason behind half of all failed mergers. I like Mencius' view on all this."

Quizzical eyebrows were raised.

"A loose translation would be," Jim continued, "opportunities of divinely approved timing are less important than advantages of the target situation on the ground. And the advantages of the target situation on the ground are less important than the people acting in unison ..."

The bankers searched for a response, while the human resources director could not stifle a smirk.

———————————

The phrase 'Right Time, Right Place, People in Harmony' is a summary of a line from the great Chinese thinker Mencius, who lived 372–289 BCE.[20] It highlights an important *li* pattern: the three conditions required for a successful outcome of any venture.

Strands of Mencius' phrase originated with Sun Tzu, as recorded in his famous *Art of War*,[21] dating from about 500 BCE. This definitive military textbook was born from centuries of chaotic battling between rival states across the lands that would become China. It is still a key text in military academies in Asia and the West. In Chapter 10, Sun Tzu emphasizes that you must choose the right terrain – i.e., place – for conducting battle.

Sun Tzu's protégé, Sun Bin, developed this maxim.[22] Sun Bin said a favourable outcome could only arise by having heavenly, earthly and human advantages. This meant, respectively, good conditions, right terrain and unified troops. His thinking mirrored the growing belief that the cosmos was made up of three parts: Heaven, Man and Earth.

———————————

20  Mengzi, *Gong Sun Chou* 2, Chapter 10.

21  Sun Tzu, *The Art of War*, Chapter 10.

22  Sun Bin, *The Art of Warfare*, Chapter 6.

Mencius lived several centuries later, in a slightly more settled era. He became counsellor to various rulers. As society became more complex, this importance of the united human factor became more important. Mencius followed the lead of Confucius in placing prime emphasis upon the people factor.

The final character of the phrase is 和 (*he*: harmony, union, together with, peace). I love its etymology: 口 (mouth) suggests the meaning (as in speaking as one, or singing in unison), while 禾 suggests the sound. But 禾 also means grain or rice – so I like to think of it as 'the unison of people eating together.' This parallels the English 'companion' that means eating bread together. This final *chengyu* on *li* patterns therefore stresses the vital importance of coordinating actions, and the leader's role in building cohesion and collaboration in the troops or team.

---

This maxim is a useful reminder of patterns of success both for leaders and for any of us in daily life, as we plan larger ventures.

First, it is a great **checklist to ensure our pattern recognition has considered all the relevant factors:**

i) Right time: the cosmos does not always organize itself to our convenience! Is this the right time to be launching something, or might there be a better time? Business leaders often consider these wider dynamics under the six headings of PESTLE: Political, Economic, Social, Technological, Legal and Environmental.

ii) Right place. You might have a great idea, but are you launching it in a place where the 'terrain' is favourable to you? No dangerous cliffs, narrow passes, marshy ground? For a business, this may relate to choosing a favourable country or market segment. In our personal lives, this may be as simple as asking whether you have chosen the right physical location to have a difficult conversation with someone. Place has power.

iii) People in harmony. Have I assembled the right team? Do they have a common direction? Have I created the conditions for them to co—operate with each other, while avoiding the pitfall of groupthink?

Second, the phrase prompts us to **consider what aspects of the unfolding pattern we can and cannot control.** Some environmental forces are beyond our control, and all we can do is to discern whether the forces are pointing in a favourable direction, given our intended timing. This is highlighted by the first character of the phrase, 天, which means ordained by Heaven or the cosmos: not merely 'right' time but heavenly or perfect timing.

Other factors, such as right place, are under our control to only a limited extent. The terrain is pre-existing, but we have a choice. We can take the high road or the low road, the scenic route or the direct route.

We have greater scope to influence other aspects of the situation (such as people in harmony) toward a favourable outcome. We can influence the outcome through, for example, team selection and motivation, and team protocols.

Third, if we accept the emphasis on people-harmony asserted by Mencius, the phrase reminds us to **prioritize our pattern recognition regarding the human dimension** as we develop our plans or as we act spontaneously. It sounds obvious, but in the hurly-burly of business life, the people factor often receives insufficient attention.

Successful business leaders and thinkers exhort us to rectify this imbalance. "First Who, then What," advises Jim Collins in his bestseller *Good to Great*, which has sold 4 million copies.[23] This is an extreme view, but he emphasizes its importance as the pace of change accelerates, both at work and in our personal lives. Before we figure out where to drive the bus, we must have the right people on it. We will probably need to change our destination ... and having the right people on the bus is the only way to choose that new direction wisely.

"Culture eats strategy for breakfast," is a phrase often attributed to Peter Drucker, recipient of the US Presidential Medal of Freedom, Japan's Order of the Sacred Treasure and other awards for his work on leadership. His assertion echoes that of Jim Collins. It also draws us beyond the selection of the right individuals, to consider how we create the conditions for excellent interaction between them. This applies to the organization, team or even family.

Culture is the set of beliefs, values, expectations and practices that guide and inform the actions of all team members. It often manifests through the team's or company's rituals, symbols, feted heroes, celebrated events and praised role models.

Culture is important for many reasons. Carolyn Dewar, senior partner at McKinsey, suggests four of them.[24] First, culture correlates with performance: companies with top quartile cultures achieve a return to shareholders 60% higher than average companies. Second, culture is very difficult to copy. A healthy culture is perhaps the most unique and enduring form of competitive advantage. Third, healthy cultures enable organizations to adapt more quickly. Fourth, unhealthy cultures lead to underperformance ... or worse. Over time, not only do unhealthy cultures foster lacklustre performance, but they can be your undoing. As daily headlines attest, culture can bring corporate giants to their knees.

---

23  Collins, *Good to Great*.

24  Dewar, "Culture: 4 Keys to Why It Matters."

Clearly there is no single 'right' culture, but researchers at Harvard Business School offer an interesting map of options. They identify two underlying aspects of culture. The first is how people respond to change (flexibility versus stability). The second is how they interact with each other (independently versus interdependently). Based on this, they go on to describe eight typical cultures. Each has a focus: Learning, Purpose, Caring, Order, Safety, Authority, Results and Enjoyment.[25]

---

**RECAP**

*Right Time, Right Place, People in Harmony* is an advanced form of *li* pattern recognition. It has proved to be a valuable maxim for millennia. It can prompt you to:

* **Manage risk in your projects and in life more generally** – by considering the factor of time, place and team.
* **Consider your timing of initiatives** – by reflecting on the degree to which the different factors can be controlled. This is akin to the well-known Serenity Prayer about accepting the things you cannot change, changing the things you can and being wise enough to distinguish between these situations. The Chinese phrase gets down to the specifics in a more tangible way.
* **Build more effective teams** – especially by focusing on 和 (harmony).

---

25  Groysberg, Lee, Price and Cheng, "The Leader's Guide to Corporate Culture."

# EXPLORING THE MAXIM

1. Reflect: What aspects of this maxim resonated most with me?

.
.
.
.
.
.

2. Consider: Where and how could this maxim help me right now?

.
.
.
.
.

3. Plan (optional): Define a relevant goal and how to get there *

GOAL: *specific goal related to focus area: measurable, achievable*

.

REALITY: *where I am on achieving this goal: evidence from present / past*

.
.

OPTIONS: *3-4 different options to achieve my goal*

.
.
.

WAY FORWARD: *Chosen option: first step, by when, support needed*

.
.
.

*See Chapter 17 for a worked example of using this GROW method.

自 然
ziran

# PRINCIPLE 3

# *ZIRAN*
# (SELF-SO-NESS)

ACT IN ACCORD WITH YOURSELF AND THE COSMOS ...
TO REALIZE YOUR FULL POTENTIAL

*Ziran* is often translated as 'just-so-ness,' 'just as it is,' 'naturally and intrinsically so,' or 'self-so-ness.' The Chinese character is a compound word 自然. It combines 自 *zi* (self; oneself; naturally; surely) with 然 *ran* (correct; right; so; thus; like this).[26] It is used as a noun, adjective and adverb – so it indicates the just-so-ness of the world and ourselves; and also the just-so-ness of how we act. It also implies 'just-as-it-should-be-ness' (according to how the cosmos works rather than what is ordained by a society or law).

Inspired by this, the Daoist believes it is better to work with things rather than against them. And it is best to do so in a way that is true both to the way the world works,

---

26 自 is a pictograph of a nose; Chinese people may point to their nose when referring to themselves. There are several interpretations of 然 – including, speculatively, that it represents a dog being sacrificed over fire, and since the dog represents rational instincts, to sacrifice it would imply eliminating irrationality and returning to a state of everything-just-as-it-should-be-ness.

and also to your own true nature. Don't try to be too smart and think you can outwit everyone and everything! By attending to the natural ways of things, we experience greater calmness, creativity, growth and flow.

*Ziran* is a multifaceted concept – so don't worry if you don't get it immediately. But it is a central part of Daoism, so it's worth persevering.

To simplify: acting with *ziran* has three aspects. First, we need to understand the *ziran* of the forces that are at work in our cosmos, and act in cognisance of them, to our advantage. The concepts of *yin-yang* (energies) and *li* (patterns), as discussed above, can help us do that.

In perceiving these forces, the Daoist views the world as an organism. The Western view arguably has seen the world more as a mechanism. Western philosophy, since Aristotle, Newton and Descartes, has seen events unfold in a chain of causes and effects. In contrast, the Daoist sees things as arising mutually, simultaneously and spontaneously ('did the mountain create the river or the river create the mountain?'). The Daoist is, therefore, more alert to the risk of unintended consequences if action is overly forced and out of tune with the cosmos and its timing.

Rather than 'pushing the river,' the Daoist favours 'using the river' ... or even 'being the river.' More enlightened modern leaders and coaches often use this principle. They find it more effective to draw in, nudge and tempt the team in ways that amplify people's 'flow.' Forcing a change in course, through directive instructions, is rarely sustainable.

Second, *ziran* requires that we understand our own true nature and act in accord with it, as part of the *ziran* of the cosmos. Our 'own true nature' is our core set of potential, energy, values, etc. that could manifest when we have discarded as many as possible of the anxieties, preconceptions and other detritus that we have built up over the years. This is clearly related to the idea of *pu* (the simplicity of the 'uncarved block'), the principle we shall explore in Principle 4 (Simplicity).

Third, *ziran* implies spontaneity. If we know the world, and we know ourselves, we can act with spontaneity. Spontaneity means to naturally act in an authentic way – rather than agonizing over decisions, dwelling on past 'mistakes,' dithering as we miss the right moment to act or reacting with a whimsical knee-jerk.

Alan Watts was a leading expositor of Daoism. In his excellent book *Tao: The Watercourse Way*, he first quotes *Daodejing*, then comments on *ziran*:

> The Tao loves and nourishes all things, but does not lord it over them. So, in the same way, the government of the body and psyche must not be egocentric. The senses, feelings and thoughts must be allowed to be spontaneous (*ziran*) in the faith that they will then order themselves harmoniously. To try to control the mind forcefully is like trying to flatten out waves with a board, and can only result in more and more disturbance.

———————

*Ziran* is a fundamental aspect of the Daoist way. In some senses, *ziran* guides the Dao. To again quote verse 25 of *Daodejing*:

> Humanity follows the Earth.
> Earth follows Heaven.
> Heaven follows the Dao.
> The Dao follows only itself-ness (*ziran*).

In daily life, this *ziran* has two related faces. It represents the self-so-ness of the way in which the world naturally works, including how events generally unfold. But it also represents the way we naturally act as an individual. This includes the 'should' of acting in harmony with the cosmos, and also the 'is' of how we do in fact act.

Percy Bysshe Shelley gives an extreme version of the way the world naturally springs back into its natural way of working, despite all our efforts as we contrive to wrestle it into a different shape. In his poem *Ozymandias*, a traveller from an antique land talks of two vast and trunkless legs of stone standing in the desert. A shattered stone head lies nearby. The narrator quotes the inscription on the plinth, then comments on it:

> "My name is Ozymandias, King of Kings;
> Look on my Works, ye Mighty, and despair!"
> Nothing beside remains. Round the decay
> Of that colossal Wreck, boundless and bare
> The lone and level sands stretch far away.[27]

The arts offer happier and more productive examples of how we can tag along with *ziran*. Painters and sculptors often have an eye for how to tap into the natural self-so-ness of nature. As mentioned earlier, Michelangelo famously saw his role as releasing the angel that already posed naturally within a block of marble. This was in contrast to chipping and chiselling away to some preplanned scheme that he might have tried to impose upon it. He employed further techniques to gain inspiration from nature. When painting, for example, he would lay a canvas against a rock and splatter paint on it. The basic contours of a convincing landscape painting would emerge, just naturally, with *ziran*, in flow.

---

27  Shelley, *The Complete Poetical Works*, 546-49.

Bob Ross was one of the most followed art teachers on TV in the 1980s and 90s. In almost every episode of his *The Joy of Painting* series he would say, "... we don't make mistakes, just happy little accidents," as he deftly turned an accidental smudge into a perfect pine tree.

In these examples from the arts, we gain an inkling of this aspect of *ziran*: spontaneity. The world, of course, acts spontaneously, but we can too – when we are in flow. One of the main messages of Laozi and the Daoists is to limit or eradicate our contrived views and practices, which deny *ziran*, and then to return to the natural and spontaneous way. Conceptually, this *ziran* and its energizing *yin-yang* are often most visible in the *li* (patterns and principles) that we covered in Principle 2 (Patterns).

## BENEFITS AND YOUR DEVELOPMENT

The benefits of acting with more *ziran* include spending less time and effort in the overthinking and overanalysing into which Google and our other modern technologies can lure us; achieving more innovative results by tapping into the vast reservoir of intuition that we know intuitively (!), can help us; and getting things right first time, by being cognisant of the fundamental *ziran* self-so-ness of a situation with which we are involved.

For the true Daoist, though, it's simpler than that: acting *ziran* is just the authentic thing to do.

To gain these benefits, try to:

First, **stop overthinking.** One of the biggest enemies of natural spontaneity is overthinking. This is a hard one for most people to tackle, and it is virtually impossible to address head-on. The more we think about not thinking, the more we think ...

We examine this in more detail in the next principle, *pu* (simplicity). But simple tips can work. These include switching to a new activity that takes blood flow and energy away from your brain's CPU – your prefrontal cortex. Such substitute activities include going for a jog, listening to music and meditating. For this to work, you will also need a cue – an alert that flashes up and tells you that it's time to switch activity. The simplest version of an alert is to decide how much time you will spend on a brain-hungry activity, and literally set a timer to tell you when to stop.

Second, **practice and honour your intuition.** Another way to suspend your potentially cumbersome and biased rational thinking is to tap into your other thinking mode – your intuition. As Alan Watts said, quoted by Marta Sinclair in *Handbook of Research Methods on Intuition,* "So long as the conscious intellect is frantically trying to clutch the world in its net of abstractions … the mood of Taoism will remain incomprehensible; and the intellect will wear itself out."[28] A good way to use your intuition more is by engaging in the reflections suggested in this book.

Third: OK, if you *really* can't stop your deliberate thinking, at least **consider things from a radically new angle.** Using metaphors and analogies is a great way to do this. Metaphors from nature can be particularly helpful, as these tap into the integrity of self-so-ness. We have already seen examples used by artists Michelangelo and Bob Ross. Extended examples from nature appear later in this book, including biomimicry, described in Chapter 17 (*Carp Leaps Dragon Gate*).

A recurring warning in Daoism is that we often get in our own way. We make things more difficult for ourselves than they need to be. That denies us the power of *ziran*.

---

28  Watts, *The Way of Zen*, 35.

# THE MAXIMS AND STORIES

In the following three chapters, *Go with Unfolding Nature* shares a collection of classical Daoist stories that get to the heart of *ziran*. *Legs Akimbo, Practically Naked* offers a vivid portrayal of spontaneity. *Calculated Waiting* illustrates how spontaneity does not necessarily mean moving quickly – and indeed how waiting in a productive way can sometimes be more *ziran*.

As you read these stories, it is useful to ask yourself:

- In what situations am I typically at my most / least spontaneous and natural?
- When I last contrived to act *against* the naturalness of a situation, was I successful or did the local cosmos spring back to its just-so state?
- When I last succeeded by working *with* the naturalness of a situation, did the related concepts of *yin-yang* energy flows and *li* patterns have a bearing?

After reading the stories, you might decide you want to develop some aspect of your own *ziran* self-so-ness and naturalness. If so, use the template following each story to help you plan your development.

# 順 其 自 然

shen qi ziran

# 7. GO WITH UNFOLDING NATURE

Gaining inspiration from
the *ziran* of the natural world

On the 6 December 2021, *Nature* – one of the world's most highly rated scientific journals – carried the story of a super jelly. This fabricated gel 'springs back' to its original state after being heavily compressed. You can squash a square inch of it with the weight of four SUV cars, 12 times over, and it will still spring back to its original state within two minutes.

This 'springing back' in a spontaneous way is one example of the natural *ziran* of the physical world.

———

The Daoists advise us to learn directly from nature, so I started this chapter with a story about *ziran* (natural self-so-ness) taken from nature itself, rather than from the classical texts of Daoism.

In the two subsequent chapters, we see the more subtle ways that *ziran* appears in the individual self, and in society.

But in this chapter we limber up in preparation, by seeing how *ziran* operates in tangible ways in the physical world. These examples offer powerful metaphors for how *ziran* operates in the person. Below I include illustrations from the fields of materials science, physical dynamics and emergence, then offer a summary of the themes. I conclude with the Daoist model of the *ziran* of the cosmos.

Our goal here is to get a feel for natural processes, observable in nature, that will inform aspects of how we ourselves co—operate with each other and our environment. Examples of these processes include 'springing back,' 'diffusing,' 'returning to equilibrium' and 'self-organizing.' The examples, of course, are selective. You can read about more complex examples elsewhere.[29]

**Material science.** Examples abound of how nature operates in a spontaneous, *ziran*, way in the material world. Ice melts, sugar dissolves in coffee, iron rusts, smells spread, puddles evaporate. These are all examples of diffusion – where substances intermingle by the natural movement of their particles. (Principle 6 will examine how you can diffuse your Self through your words or charismatic presence.)

Other examples of *ziran* demonstrate elasticity. The super-gel springs back when the weight of the four SUVs is removed, bamboo bends then straightens. A steel bar bends then whips back, an archer's stretched bow unbends. Here we see a springing-back-ness, when a body returns to its original shape and size as the forces causing the deformation are removed. Everything is a bit elastic, and everything has its elastic limit – after which it will either remain in its extended state (think 'ductile') or, of course, break (think 'stiff').

---

29 See, for example: https://plato.stanford.edu/entries/properties-emergent/.

**Other materials properties.** A range of other properties have their own type of *ziran*: strength, toughness, hardness, hardenability, brittleness, malleability, ductility, creep and slip.

Some processes reflect substantial transformation of the material – such as $H^2O$ changing from ice to water to gas. As mentioned earlier, these are called phase changes. Other examples of phase transitions include molten carbon changing to diamonds at the right temperature and pressure. Often the transition is between solid, liquid and gas. But transitions between other states – including crystalline, colloid, glassy, amorphous and plasma – are possible too.

With a bit of imagination, you can see how these properties and phase changes have analogies in the *ziran* of the human self. These include the phase transitions from calm to angry, and from the placid protest group that flips and becomes an angry mob.

**Physical dynamics.** *Ziran* naturalness is manifest in dynamic systems, not just the largely static examples cited above. Pendulums swing, ripples radiate, planets spin, seasons return, tides ebb and flow. Often these dynamics are regular rhythms; sometimes irregular ones.

Other types of natural dynamics are hidden, yet no less beautiful when revealed. One of my favourites, and the one that led me to study theoretical physics at the University of Cambridge, is the so-called brachistochrone curve, or path of fastest descent. Galileo came up with an erroneous solution, but Newton solved it in a single night of hard work. It attracted the attention of other brilliant mathematicians too, such as Bernoulli and Leibnitz. The exam question was: Given two points A and B (with A not directly above B), what is the shape of the curve that allows a frictionless object to slide between A and B in the *shortest possible* time?

That path of fastest descent turns out to be a cycloid, regardless of the relative positions of points A and B. This is the curved path traced by a point on the rim of a bike's wheel as you ride it. Somewhat amazingly, it turns out that from *whatever* point you release the object – from higher up on the slide, or lower down – it always takes *the same amount of time* to reach the bottom.

Mechanisms like these lurk deep within our natural world, and hint at the dynamics of our broader environments.

**Emergence.** A set of entirely different examples of the natural *ziran* workings of the cosmos comes from the arena called emergence, or emergent behaviour. There is a similar underlying magic for the reasons birds flock, the clumping of cars shifts up and down a traffic jam, sand dunes form and shift, ants develop the shortest path routes (through depositing ephemeral pheromones), tigers develop stripes and a living brain emerges from a couple of cells.

These systems are said to show emergent properties when 'the whole is greater than the sum of its parts.' In other words, the look and behaviour of the collective group is very different from those of its individual components. This can happen whether those components are cells, grains of sand or insects.

'Emergent features' also appear in the dynamics of social networks. These features underpin why your TikTok video goes viral, and why you are linked to most other people on the planet with only a few degrees of separation. It's just *ziran* – the way things naturally are – and hence often translated as self-so-ness!

---

**Wuxing.** The Daoists had a 'theory of everything.' It reflected the natural *ziran* processes of both the external world and our internal bodies and psyches. This model is called the *wuxing*, meaning five processes. Early versions of this model were discovered in the inscriptions on the Oracle Bones that date from before 1,000 BCE, and in texts written earlier than the 3rd century BCE.[30]

The *wuxing* model represents the cosmic agents of natural change. Starting with the five elements (water, wood, fire, earth and metal), the *wuxing* represents the five processes that work in a cycle between them. For example, in its nourishing or constructive cycle, water nourishes the wood of trees, wood nourishes fire, fire creates embers and hence earth, and earth creates metal. The *wuxing* is often mistranslated as 'five elements.' This translation is incorrect because the crucial aspect of the model is the dynamic forces though which the elements interact – rather than the elements themselves.

Over time, the five elements became identified not only with planets (the five-fold symbolism of which had pre-dated the five elements described above), but also with other aspects of nature. In Traditional Chinese Medicine, these elements include aspects of the human body and of human behaviour. Later Daoist thinking identified these elements with the five cardinal virtues of wisdom, sincerity, benevolence, righteousness and reverence.

---

30  See, for example, the Internet Encyclopedia of Philosophy: https://iep.utm.edu/wuxing/.

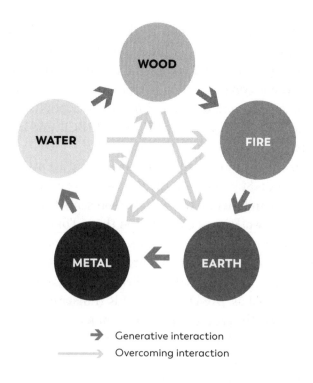

→ Generative interaction
⟶ Overcoming interaction

**WUXING - FIVE ELEMENTS OF CHANGE**

There are many further aspects of the *wuxing*, such as cycles of depletion rather than nourishing, beyond the scope of this book. I mention this model because it offers a further example of portraying the 'unfolding nature' with which we co—operate in *ziran*. It also illustrates an important bridge between our perception of the exterior world, and its metaphorical meaning for us.

To quote again from verse 25 of *Daodejing*:

Humanity follows the Earth.
Earth follows Heaven.
Heaven follows the Tao.
The Tao follows only itself.

The purpose of this chapter was to introduce *ziran* with some simple examples drawn from nature. By examining *ziran* in nature, and playing with the concept, we become more attuned to its existence. Richard Feynman, physicist and Nobel laureate who had a wicked sense of humour, recounts in his brilliant autobiography *Surely You're Joking, Mr Feynman!* how he once tried to nudge a group of ants to go around in a circle, following their own pheromone trail – a great example of exploring nature's *ziran* in a playful way.

**RECAP**

*Go With Unfolding Nature* is a maxim to remind us to sense the directions in which our cosmos and environments are moving, so that we can choose to go with them or – in full awareness – against them. Understanding *ziran* is an important factor in achieving flow. The examples in this chapter, drawn from nature, are aimed to offer a tangible and directly accessible foundation for thinking and doing *ziran*. As you reflect on how the *ziran* of nature can give insight into your own *ziran*, three questions may help you:

- **What examples and metaphors from the natural world have helped you in the past?** No aspect of life can evade the link to the physics, dynamics and *ziran* of nature – from the simple acts of breathing and walking, to the way we engage with friends and colleagues.

- **What *further* metaphors could you use?** You will find you can apply almost any aspect of nature's *ziran* to increase your creativity, reduce your anxiety or nurture other people.

- **How can you engage with the *ziran* of nature in a physical way?** Try adopting Richard Feynman's playful approach to deepen your feel for *ziran* – the self-so-ness of nature.

# EXPLORING THE MAXIM

1. Reflect: What aspects of this maxim resonated most with me?

.
.
.
.
.
.

2. Consider: Where and how could this maxim help me right now?

.
.
.
.
.

3. Plan (optional): Define a relevant goal and how to get there *

GOAL: *specific goal related to focus area: measurable, achievable*
.

REALITY: *where I am on achieving this goal: evidence from present / past*
.
.

OPTIONS: *3-4 different options to achieve my goal*
.
.
.

WAY FORWARD: *Chosen option: first step, by when, support needed*
.
.
.

*See Chapter 17 for a worked example of using this GROW method.

# 解 衣 般 礴, 裸

jie yi ban bo, luo

# 8. LEGS AKIMBO, PRACTICALLY NAKED

Finding personal *ziran*
to live in authentic spontaneity

Duke Yuan of Song wanted some pictures painted, and all the painting masters gathered. They received instructions and bowed, then stood in line, licking their brushes and mixing their ink. There were so many of them that half of them had to stand outside. One painter came late. Leisurely and in no particular hurry, he received his instructions and bowed.

But this painter did not bother to stand in line, and instead headed off to the living quarters. The Duke sent someone to fetch him. And when they eventually found him, there he was with most of his clothes off. He was sitting on the floor and painting away, legs akimbo, cross-legged, practically naked.

When Lord Song heard of this, he said, "Excellent! At last we have found a true painter."

---

The prior chapter illustrated *ziran* natural self-so-ness in the non-human world. This chapter moves on to show how the person, symbolized by the artist, lives their authentic self-so-ness. This is another wonderful story from the ancient Daoist classic *Zhuangzi* (section 12.7), in which the author gives many illustrations of *ziran* – natural spontaneity.

The story portrays three recurring aspects of Daoist *ziran*, which are presented widely across the classics of *Daodejing*, *Zhuangzi* and *Liezi*. Firstly is your refusal to be constrained by convention. You don't make a big deal of it, and instead you just focus on 'it's what I do.' The story emphasizes this through the artist not standing in line. Secondly is your discarding of the obstacles that might impede the free-flowing performance of your art. The story shows this as the discarding of clothes. Of course, this stands metaphorically for discarding the constraints of filters and prejudices behind which we normally operate. The third aspect portrayed is, nevertheless, the spirited engagement with life. After all, the artist was not a recluse: he did make the effort to turn up, and did make time to receive the instructions.

The story therefore helps deal with misconceptions that can arise when *ziran* is translated as 'spontaneity,' as it frequently is. There are nuances here that are subtle but important, so please bear with the brief excursion into etymology ...

The English word 'spontaneity' derives from the Latin *sua sponte,* meaning 'of your own free will.' This works well as a translation for *ziran* – provided that 'will' is read as something like 'what I will myself to do, driven not merely by my whim in the moment, but by my quintessential heart-mind that is engaged with the cosmos.' Therefore, it is close to Heidegger's notion of *dasein* (German for 'being-and-doing-there-ness'). *Ziran* also aligns with other synonyms of 'spontaneous' – such as being natural, instinctual, uncontrived, volitional and unconstrained.

But the English word 'spontaneity' also has negative connotations, as any dictionary or thesaurus will show. These can give a superficial or warped view of what *ziran* is. Treacherous synonyms for 'spontaneous' are therefore words like 'impulsive' (OK if the impulse is understood to emanate from the polished mirror of clear perception; not OK if it is read as an impulse driven merely by a fight-or-flight reaction fuelled by adrenaline); or 'spur of the moment' (OK if this spur is the 'echo' in *Zhuangzi*'s 'move like water, mind as mirror, respond like an echo'; not OK if it is read as merely 'whimsical').

To avoid all this wordsmithing, the Daoists luckily offer us more tangible illustrations of *ziran*.

**Spirit resonance, life motion.** In the mid-6th century, the painter Xie He compiled the earliest known Chinese work on the theory of art. In his *Classification of Painters of Former Times (Gu Huapin Lu)*, he reviews the works of 27 renowned painters.[31] He then distils six aesthetic principles by which any painting should be judged. His principles had a lasting impact for many centuries.

The first principle he lists is 'spirit resonance, life motion' (the four-character phrase *qi yun sheng dong*). This was considered the most important principle of Chinese painting. If you did not get that principle, you need not bother trying to be a painter.

The exact meaning of the phrase is still debated. At its core, however, is the sense that the spirit of any great painter resonates, dynamically and in harmony, with the spirit of nature. This endows the painter's work with life and movement. In creating this microcosm, the artist is not merely recording the view of a landscape; at a metaphysical

---

31  Xie He 謝赫, Gu Huapin Lu 古畫品錄, *Siku Quanshu* vol. 812, 1b.

level, the artist is also creating something that will interact with the macrocosm in a two-way exchange of *qi*.

We succeed in the art of painting, and in the art of living, only if we co—operate our natural *ziran* self-so-ness with that of the cosmos.

**Double dragons play with pearl.** The practices of the qigong school of wellness offer us a view of *ziran* from a slightly different angle. Qigong is a school of movements to promote health. In many ways, it is similar to the more widely known tai chi. Although qigong is not exclusively Daoist, the two systems share many principles. One of qigong's sequences is called *Double Dragons Play with Pearl.*[32] Its movements, visualizations and breathing routines aim to encourage the flow of *qi* (vital energy).

It is the name of the sequence that offers a further window onto the elusive concept of *ziran*. Here, the two 'contending dragons' at play represent our internal *yin-yang* creative energies that we met in earlier chapters. They also represent terrestrial and celestial powers, respectively. The pearl with which they play symbolizes wisdom, perfection and enlightenment.

Thus, the movement's name reminds us that being *ziran* is to move in the world in a flowing and playful way. This is a way in which the varied (and varying) *yin-yang* energies of our Selves and of the cosmos create enlightenment for us and for the myriad things. It is a valuable mantra for the qigong practitioner and the layman alike.

**The years like great black oxen tread the world.** To give the Western reader a brief break from the oriental examples, I offer as a last illustration a verse from R.B. Yeats' play *The Countess Cathleen*. It runs:

---

32  See, for example: Wu, *Vital Breath of the Dao: Chinese Shamanic Tiger Qigong*, 177.

> The years like great black oxen tread the world
> And God, the herdsman, goads them on behind.[33]

(Yeats concludes with the line "And I am trampled by their passing feet," but the more joyful reader may replace this with something more positive!)

Here we see time drawn onwards inexorably by those big black oxen. This reminds us that the *ziran* self-so-ness of the cosmos moves at its own speed. That speed may differ from our immediate needs, and we do well to recognize that. The way that *ziran* self-so-ness works across time, and its implications for us, are portrayed in more detail in Principle 5 (Effortless Action), where we explore *wuwei*.

---

**RECAP**

*Ziran* is a cornerstone of the Daoist way. It is the natural, quintessential, innate way in which we, and the cosmos, work in space and over time. It might sound easy to align ourselves to co—operate with nature but, as we will see, this requires dissolving our deeply engrained prejudices, filters and dysfunctional desires, to achieve *pu* simplicity (Principle 4), so we can then operate in *wuwei* effortless action (Principle 5).

*Legs Akimbo, Practically Naked* is a powerful reminder of how we can live in a way that is quintessentially natural to our selves.

---

33  Yeats, *Poems*, "The Countess Cathleen" Act 4.

# EXPLORING THE MAXIM

1.  Reflect: What aspects of this maxim resonated most with me?

    .
    .
    .
    .
    .
    .

2.  Consider: Where and how could this maxim help me right now?

    .
    .
    .
    .
    .

3.  Plan (optional): Define a relevant goal and how to get there *

    GOAL: *specific goal related to focus area: measurable, achievable*

    .

    REALITY: *where I am on achieving this goal: evidence from present / past*

    .
    .
    .

    OPTIONS: *3-4 different options to achieve my goal*

    .
    .
    .

    WAY FORWARD: *Chosen option: first step, by when, support needed*

    .
    .
    .

*See Chapter 17 for a worked example of using this GROW method.

NOTES

# 9. CALCULATED WAITING

Mining the *I Ching*'s rich insights
to make better decisions


Marco strides nimbly into the room for our coaching session. He is the chief financial officer of a very large bank. He has been trying to build a better relationship with his boss, Bill, the bank's chief executive. Marco has a forceful personality, and is an expert in risk management. He always delivers ahead of schedule: he sees his winning formula as 'speed.' Marco had chosen to get a coach – he had no pressure from HR. Nevertheless, our first three sessions have made little progress. Marco wants an agenda and wants to frogmarch through it. Our sessions feel hurried.

I have a new game plan in mind. But I quickly discard it as Marco surprises me. "We need a new approach," he starts. "My daughter is studying in China. She WeChatted me this morning and made me promise to give the *I Ching* a try. Have you heard of it?"

"You mean the ancient book of Chinese wisdom?" I venture. "Supposed to be the oldest book in the world?"

"Yes," replies Marco. "That one. Not really my cup of tea, but I promised my daughter, so I guess I'd better give it a go. I realize it's not a prediction machine, but perhaps it can help me solve my problem."

"OK," I reply, "if you're really sure …"

You start a consultation with the *Yijing* (aka *I Ching*) by having a clear question in mind. Then you write it down so you are committed to it, and then you pause to reflect on it. Marco surprises me again by saying he's been offered a job at another bank, and wants to know whether to take it. It pays less. This other bank has a weaker brand. But at least he would not have to work with Bill.

Yes/no questions do not provoke the *Yijing*'s deepest insights, so Marco reframes his inquiry. "How should I approach my decision to switch jobs?"

First we create a hexagram. A hexagram is a simple symbol of six stacked lines that are either solid or broken. Though simple in form, the hexagrams are endowed with many layers of meaning. We start the random process to create the hexagram for the inquiry that Marco posed. Marco finds three coins and drops them on the desk: two heads and a tail. I glance at the crib-sheet on my phone. It tells me that I should draw this coin combination as a single unbroken line. This is the lowest of the hexagram's six lines. The next two lines come out the same, so the bottom half of the hexagram consists of three unbroken lines. I mention that this represents Creative Power; then we continue. The next toss falls as three heads, so I draw a broken line with a dot next to it. A solid line is next, and then a broken line.

I glance at another crib-sheet on my phone, to read off the interpretation.

I clear my throat, wondering how Mr Speedy will like what he is about to hear. "As I said, the lower three lines represent Creative Power." Marco seems to like that. "The upper three lines represent Water," I continue. "Together they are Hexagram 5 – Calculated Waiting."

"Waiting? Waiting?" asks Marco, starting to fidget. "That's the very last thing I want to do. There must be some mistake. I need to make a decision now!"

I persuade Marco to at least hear the interpretation – I remind him that he had promised his daughter.

The *I Ching* tells us that 'Creative Power in the lower trigram is held in check by the profound mystery of Water above.' Forces beyond your knowledge are at work. You can make no purposeful progress right now. This is a good time to relax and gain perspective on the situation. But use the time to learn more and discern other options. That is why it is *calculated* waiting – not just waiting.

I ask Marco what meaning he chooses to assign to this, and he gradually warms to the adventure of exploring its relevance.

Then he asks about the dot I drew next to the fourth line up. That indicates a 'changing line.' Hexagram 5 tells of the current situation, but a changing line offers a further insight. We read the interpretation of line 4 changing. The *I Ching* text asks whether Marco could be at the centre of a particularly chaotic situation. If so, he should consider removing himself from it immediately!

We explore how this could be relevant for Marco, and then he asks whether there are any pointers for the future. To unveil this, we take Hexagram 5 and change the broken 'changing line' 4 to a solid line. This generates a new hexagram.

I go on to explain that this new sign is Hexagram 43 – 'Resolution.' This signifies the same Creative Power below, but now stimulating the Lake above. This symbolizes that the situation will be brought to openness and fruition.

"Fruition?" asks Marco. "Sounds better than Calculated Waiting. But what on Earth could Fruition mean?"

"You tell me – what does it mean for you?" I counter.

We pause, blinking at each other.

"No idea," he continues. "Fruition? I guess it means I take that other job even though I don't really want it ..."

"OK ... any other meanings?

"Fruition?" he repeats, "perhaps Bill changes his behaviour and we start to work better together?"

"Yes, or ...?"

Marco glances at his watch, but I press him one more time for his interpretation. "I really don't know," he says. "But these ideas have registered. As you know, I do like the *Calculated* bit, even if I don't like the *Waiting* bit. I guess I'll spin the head-hunters out for a few more weeks on the other job. I'll spend more time with our board of directors – in case they are the 'unknown forces at work'..." He smiles and leaves.

Two weeks later, Marco calls me. "You'll never guess," he teases. "You'll never guess ... I found out what Fruition meant."

He was clearly going to tell me anyway, but I played along, "... and ...?"

"Bill just got fired! Now the board wants me to apply for the job to replace him as chief executive. Lucky that I hadn't rushed to accept that other lousy job. Calculated Waiting ... I like it."

[Here ends a true story.]

———————

This story highlights one of the main messages of the *Yijing*: that the cosmos moves at its own speed. It will not change pace just for your own convenience. It advises you to pay close attention to the timing in any situation.

The *Yijing* is the crystallized wisdom of the sages of ancient China. It is a powerful tool that can offer you unusual insights. If you are wedded to more conventional ways to address problems or opportunities, then you may feel reluctant to consult the *Yijing*. In that case, please remember to try it out when your familiar techniques fail!

Over the course of several millennia, the *Yijing* built into a storehouse of perceptions about how to deal with challenging situations or opportunities. Scholars still debate its precise origins. But all agree that it grew from a humble start.

The *Yijing* likely evolved from divinatory tools used 3,000–4,000 years ago. Superstitious farmers sought signs from the spirit-gods – for example, was this a good time to plant crops? Throwing coloured or notched stalks taken from the yarrow bush, they sought a thumbs-up sign of *yang*, or a thumbs-down sign of *yin*. They used what was a single line of what we now call a hexagram.

As the early farmers faced more complex situations, they needed a broader range of outcomes. Using two lines could offer four outcomes, just as tossing coins does. Three lines could offer eight interpretations. Eventually the three-lined trigrams were formed. They became iconic symbols of powerful concepts: Heaven, Earth, Water, Fire, Wind, Thunder, Mountain and Lake. The 64 hexagrams then emerged by joining an upper trigram to a lower one. Including the changing lines, 4,096 different responses are possible.

Traditionally, four great sages recorded the meanings of the hexagrams and their individual lines: the legendary

Fu Hsi; King Wen; the Duke of Chou; and Confucius. King Wen was the forebear of the Chou Dynasty, reigning from 1171–1122 BCE. Scholars believe he developed the 64 hexagrams from the eight trigrams invented by Fu Hsi. He may also have added brief judgments to the hexagrams, written while imprisoned by a tyrant.

This useful aid to thinking slowly gained ground. Ancient narratives record more than 20 professional divinations conducted for royal families between 671 BCE and 487 BCE. Influential commentaries developed and were absorbed into the book. The *I Ching* could now address a far broader range of situations then the earlier casters of the yarrow sticks could have imagined.

Several themes run through the *Yijing*, and most of them relate to *ziran* self-so-ness. The first theme is the '**three potencies**': the cosmos consists of Heaven and Earth, and Mankind in between them. These three realms are intrinsically interwoven with each other. As mankind, we can try to be the prime mover, but the empire (Heaven and Earth) will always strike back. The second theme is **change** and how we deal with it … or embrace it. *Yin* is always changing to *yang* and vice versa, and the uncertainty can cause us fear and anxiety. The *Yijing* offers us pointers to what we might want to consider before acting. The third theme is a **hierarchy of factors** to consider in any situation. These range from instincts (the lowest line of the hexagram), through self-interest, individual endeavours, social consciousness, authority and wisdom (the top line to the hexagram). If you are familiar with Abraham Maslow's well-known 'Hierarchy of Needs,' you will notice a resemblance. Maslow records his interest in Daoism, for example, talking of "the concept of motivated, purposeful spontaneity of Taoistic (Daoistic) yielding and letting go."[34]

The value of the *Yijing* is well-summarized by scholar John Minford. He spent ten years translating the book into

Penguin's English edition. He concluded that the *I Ching* triggers lateral thinking, offering a way out of habitual, unhelpful patterns of thought.

--------------------

Five tips for consulting the *I Ching* are:

First, find an **accessible but reliable edition**. I recommend R.L. Wing's *The I Ching Workbook*. It is deep enough, but not too elaborate. Its layout makes for easy reading. Its spiral binding lets you lay the book flat to jot notes in it. Wing points out that you, the reader, are the investigator and that the experiments you make with the *Yijing* will give you a better understanding "of the cosmos and your Self, one and the same."[35] I avoid online sites that automatically generate an interpretation, since they tend to be glib.

Second, consult the *Yijing*, initially, on **situations in which you are open to 'unusual' insights**. Avoid using it initially on a life-changing issue, as you will lack sufficient familiarity with the book.

Third, pose your **question carefully**. Wing's book offers guidelines. Avoid questions with yes/no answers. For example, not 'Should I take this new job?' Rather 'What should I pay attention to as I explore this upcoming decision?' Or, 'What could I expect from making the job switch?'

Fourth, **avoid wishful interpretation**! It's tempting to pay more attention to those aspects of the reading that appeal most. Give equal weight to its observations that might superficially seem less appealing.

--------------------

34  Maslow, *Motivation and Personality*. 133.

35  Wing, *The I Ching Workbook*, back cover.

Finally, **reflect on the *Yijing*'s value to you**. Take notes. Consult the *Yijing* at least a few times for differing situations. See the patterns that are useful to you. Record the dates of your readings, as you are likely to refer back to the notes several years later.

---

**RECAP**

The *Yijing* embodies millennia of reflection on how we make decisions. It can help you make more considered decisions by confronting you with aspects that you might have overlooked. It is not a predictive tool. As scholar John Minford puts it, "*Yijing* is just a mirror, it is for you yourself to understand your life and destiny."

---

# EXPLORING THE MAXIM

1.  Reflect: What aspects of this maxim resonated most with me?

    - 
    - 
    - 
    - 
    - 
    - 

2.  Consider: Where and how could this maxim help me right now?

    - 
    - 
    - 
    - 
    - 

3.  Plan (optional): Define a relevant goal and how to get there *

    GOAL: *specific goal related to focus area: measurable, achievable*

    - 

    REALITY: *where I am on achieving this goal: evidence from present / past*

    - 
    - 
    - 

    OPTIONS: *3-4 different options to achieve my goal*

    - 
    - 
    - 

    WAY FORWARD: *Chosen option: first step, by when, support needed*

    - 
    - 
    - 

*See Chapter 17 for a worked example of using this GROW method.

樸
*pu*

# PRINCIPLE 4

# *PU*
# (SIMPLICITY)

PERCEIVE WITHOUT PREJUDICE ...
TO SEE WITH CLARITY

The word *pu* means simple, plain, honest; rough. It refers to the original unworked state of a thing. The Daoist often refers to this state – particularly the state of the nonprejudiced mind – as 'uncarved wood.' (I like to think of it as uncarved *but living* wood, rather than a block of dead wood ...)

The Chinese character for *pu* is 樸. This combines the radical for a tree 木 with that for thicket 業. This originally signified a type of oak that grew in thickets – i.e., a tree of solid lumber. While 'uncarved block' is the most frequently cited metaphor for the pristine mind, other metaphors include 'unworked silk' and 'unpolished jade.' I wonder whether this juxtaposition of tree and thicket implies 'seeing the wood from the trees' – although I doubt you'll see that assertion in any Chinese dictionary.

The goal of the *pu* principle is to keep our mind uncarved, unworked and unadorned. This means it is free from filters, biases and prejudgments. Only then do we see the unvarnished reality of our team, relationships and environment and avoid an ignorant outlook. We absorb what we see and feel without blinkering and filtering the sensory messages.

We can use our full peripheral vision and achieve our potential. But we do so only if we register what is happening in our cosmos onto a blank-slate, open mind.

Benjamin Hoff's *The Tao of Pooh*, which sat on *The New York Times* bestseller list for 49 weeks, explores this idea. Its title makes a pun of *pu* = Pooh. Using characters from A. A. Milne's Winnie the Pooh stories, it shows how Rabbit shuttles about and overthinks things yet does not accomplish much. In contrast, Pooh-bear has a more open-minded approach and often happens to find the solution to problems that the group faces, in a nondeliberate and unexpected way.

This uncarved, natural self is in accord with nature and circumstances as they unfold. We can reclaim our state of natural perception, but only if we detox. This requires dumping the detritus of our accumulated desires and attachments. Tony Robbins' acclaimed bestseller *Awaken the Giant Within* epitomizes in its title the power of giving rein – and reign – to this natural self.

It can be hard to achieve this state of *pu* simplicity in today's busy and goal-oriented world. Few of us are brave enough to spend all our time in the playfulness that best characterizes *pu* simplicity. Even the committed Daoist is not a recluse who forsakes all goals. Yet by tethering ourselves to goals that we consider immutable, we risk developing anxiety, reverting to proven yet overly grooved ways of thinking, and allowing our wishful desires to cloud our vision and interpretation. The Daoist sees goals, and goalposts, as being always in motion. At an extreme, the Daoist does not bother with the goalposts at all!

Meditation is clearly a tool to detox the filters of prejudice – and thus it is a route to *pu*-style openness and mindfulness. The Daoist master lives in this state continuously, not merely during a formal meditation session.

Enhanced creativity is one of the many benefits of a *pu* mindset. Daoism has the happy habit of plonking us in a place where we are forced to see things from a new angle. We see situations and solutions in ways that produce outcomes that are more creative and productive. Most of us are familiar with the *koans* of Zen Buddhism (for example, 'What is the sound of one hand clapping?'). Daoism, as the mother of Zen, also offers us ways to completely and utterly reframe things.

This belief is asserted in the very first verse of *Daodejing*:

> Freed from desire, you can see the hidden mystery.
> By having desire, you can only see what is visibly real.

As you might expect, Daoists see potential biases lurking in language. Even words are potentially dangerous to the 'uncarved block,' because they are a form of labelling. Words are seen as categories and labels that we attach to carved-up pixels of reality. These pixels inevitably fragment our understanding of the world into detached elements, and by focussing on the pixels we likely fail to grasp the full oil painting that is the cosmos.

––––––––––––––

This power of simplicity in perceiving and acting is emphasized by all the classic texts of Daoism. For example, verse 21 of *Daodejing* has:

> Knowing you don't know is wholeness.
> Thinking you know is a disease.

Only by recognizing that you have an illness can you move to seek a cure.

The Master is whole because she sees her illnesses and treats them, and thus is able to remain whole.

Section 4.2 of the *Zhuangzi* suggests:

Maintain a perfect unity in every movement of your will. You will not wait for the hearing of your ears about it, but for the hearing of your mind. You will not wait even for the hearing of your mind, but for the hearing of the spirit.

And in section 7.6:

When the perfect man employs his mind, it is a mirror ... It responds ... but does not retain. Thus, he is able to deal successfully with all things, and injures none.

Section 4.2 of the *Liezi* has:

My body is aligned with my mind, my mind with my energies, my energies with the cosmos, and the cosmos with the Dao. Because of this intimate union, I perceive any interference in the universal harmony – whether it comes from the eight wildernesses far away, or from between my eyebrows and my eyelashes. I can't say by which organ I perceive it. I know, without knowing how I knew.

By adopting *pu* simplicity, we see more directly into the heart of things. We also benefit from having wider perspectives; find more creative solutions to problems by connecting more dots; and increase our resilience to the world's events by reacting more swiftly and adaptably.

In all these examples, however, it is not merely the mind that is stilled, it is the *heart-mind*. This is a crucial concept. In China, cognition and emotion are seen as innately combined. Thus, the character for the heart, *xin* 心, means the heart as the seat of *emotion* and the mind as the seat of *cognition* as inextricably entwined. Daoists talk of 'fasting the heart-mind'[36] through meditation. This means quieting both the feeling and the thinking. That 'fasting' leaves the heart-mind unencumbered and, hence, perspicacious. The story of Master Liezi, in the next chapter, explains this in more detail. He freed himself so completely of prejudice and desire that he could ride with the wind.

---

For the Daoist, a common metaphor for having achieved *pu* simplicity is the mind-like-mirror. It would be easy to read this simply as the idea that a highly polished mirror will reflect external reality to us with perfect clarity, and that we should therefore cleanse our minds as we would polish a mirror.

There is, however, a further nuance. In the philosophies of China, the mirror is seen as an active responder to the environment, not merely a passive reflector.[37] Since ancient times, the Chinese used bronze mirrors to create fire and water. By concentrating the sun's rays, a mirror could start a fire. At night, the mirror would cool and condense water from the atmosphere. The mirror was thus seen as having the power to draw these *yang* and *yin* elements from the cosmos. In some sense, the polished mirror was not merely active, but actually modelled the workings of Heaven and Earth.

---

36  xin zhai 心齋

37  Cline, "Mirrors, Minds, and Metaphors."

As Cline puts it in her paper "Mirrors, Minds, and Metaphors":

> The mirror metaphor in the *Zhuangzi* is about more than the state of a person's heart-mind; it concerns the nature of the world and its relation to human beings. When one moves in accord with the Way, the need for a sense of self apart from the ten thousand things recedes, and one comes to see oneself as but a small part of the larger patterns and processes of the world. In this way, sages come to appreciate things as they really are, and rely on their spontaneous, pre-reflective intuitions for guidance ... In Chapter 13 the *Zhuangzi* calls this state the perfection of Dao and *de*. Like a mirror, the heart-mind is responsive and illuminating, but it is also still and calm.[38]

Many Daoist texts take this metaphor of mirror, and combine it with the metaphor of water. Still waters offer perfect reflection; troubled or muddied waters do not. Chapter 4 of *Zhuangzi* starts to bring all these ideas together in the mantra mentioned earlier and adopted by martial artist Bruce Lee:

> Moving, be like water.
> Still, be like a mirror.
> Respond like an echo.

Finding the polish of the mirror or the stillness of the water is not an end in itself – though many meditation courses

---

38  Cline, "Mirrors, Minds, and Metaphors."

may imply otherwise. The true value of cleansing the heart-mind is elegantly illustrated by *The Ten Ox-Herding Pictures*.

This series of small, cartoon-like paintings emerged in China during the 12ᵗʰ century. The pictures and accompanying text illustrate the stages typical of Zen meditation and gaining enlightenment. Katsuki Sekida's translation shows, in the first picture, how a young person starts the search for his own true nature – symbolized by the missing ox.[39] Pictures 2 through 6 then show his stages of development. They range from 'finding the footprints' through to 'riding the ox home.' The latter picture represents his mastery of being able to access the meditative state and being enlightened. Surprisingly, that is not the end of the story ...

Spoiler alert! Picture 7 is *Ox Lost, Man Remaining*, in which enlightenment and even Zen are seen as an irrelevant crutch and are forgotten. Even when we get to picture 8 *No Ox, no Man*, where everything has been transcended, we have still not reached the end. Picture 9 has the man *Returning to the Source*, and finally we reach picture 10 *In Town with Helping Hands*. We see a carefree, potbellied man wandering barefoot (to symbolize his mental nakedness), whose only thought is to bring joy to others. The cardinal purpose of polishing the heart-mind is to engage authentically with the world.

And, of course, the world also has its own version of *pu* simplicity. As Sir Isaac Newton said:

> Nature does nothing in vain when less will serve; for Nature is pleased with simplicity and affects not the pomp of superfluous causes.[40]

---

39 Sekida, *Zen Training: Methods and Philosophy*, Chapter 17.

40 Newton, *The Mathematical Principles of Natural Philosophy*, 160.

## BENEFITS AND YOUR DEVELOPMENT

By developing your *pu* simplicity, you will discern the world more clearly. You will see more vividly the *yin-yang* energy flows, the *li* patterns and principles, and the *ziran* self-so-ness that we encountered in earlier chapters. More specifically, you:

- Live with greater clarity, simplicity and creativity
- Be more adaptable to unexpected events
- Be less stressed

How can we achieve this *pu* simplicity of heart-mind so that we achieve these benefits and act with the *ziran* spontaneity that we saw earlier?

You have three options. These techniques are complementary – not mutually exclusive.

First, use your **preferred type of meditation to 'fast your heart-mind.'** Neuroscience shows that meditation works, even if you meditate for as little as 13 minutes. Meditation significantly enhances attention, working memory and recognition memory. It also decreases negative mood, anxiety and fatigue.[41]

There are many types of meditation. A 2019 academic paper reviewed more than 100 of them.[42] In some techniques you focus your attention: on a mantra, candle or other object or thought. In contrast, other methods include open monitoring: you stay attentive to any experience that might arise, but without selecting, judging or focusing on

---

41  Basso, "Brief, Daily Meditation Enhances Attention, Memory, Mood." Tang, "Short-Term Meditation Training Improves Attention and Self-Regulation." Tang, "Brief Mental Training Reorganizes Large-Scale Brain Networks." Lavretsky, "A Pilot Study of Yogic Meditation for Family Dementia Caregivers."

42  Matko, "What is Meditation?"

any particular object. We are not yet sure whether or how their benefits differ.

The next chapter reveals several Daoist techniques, aimed at stilling the heart-mind, so it can receive and perceive more clearly.

Second, **remove the blinkers and de-program preju-dices.** While I was studying hard at Stanford University in 1980, little did I know that a few blocks down the street, Daniel Kahneman was putting the finishing touches to a paper that would be considered the founding text of behavioural economics. Kahneman won the Nobel Prize for Economic Sciences in 2002. His 2011 bestseller, *Thinking, Fast and Slow,* explained his insights in a popular way. The book sets out the model, now widely accepted, that explains how our mind has two parallel ways of working. There is the faster, intuitive system, and the slower, more deliberate system.

Each system has its benefits. The faster system helps us escape the lion, tiger and other threats; the slower one allows us to take a logical and comprehensive view of matters. But each system has its weaknesses, too, which can smudge and warp the polished mirror of our mind. For example, the faster system can develop 'amygdala hijack' – the hair-trigger reaction we covered earlier. This can create a dysfunctionally explosive response to even the slightest threat. But the slower system can malfunction too. It can invoke our built-up filters and biases, so we turn a blind eye to reality, and thus lose our objectivity.

Meditative techniques try to dissolve both these malfunctions in a general way. In contrast, other techniques try to dismantle specific biases and preconceptions in a more laser-focused way. These latter techniques go under the title of cognitive behavioural therapy. You can use them if you know what specific type of cognitive distortion you want to address. One version uses the ABCD process. In this, you systematically first examine the **A**ctivating event that triggers your dysfunctional response. Then you discern the (fallacious) **B**elief that has caused your choice of response. Next, you explicitly log and accept the negative **C**onsequence you experience in terms of emotions. In the final crucial step, you **D**ispute and debunk some aspect of the relevant belief. Chapter 12 (*Cart South, Track North*) illustrates this highly effective process in more detail.

This sledgehammer approach is called 'cognitive behavioural therapy'. It might seem a tad un-Daoist. Nevertheless, it is a highly successful form of psychotherapy for the more extreme types of heart-mind distortion – such as anxiety, phobias and related ailments.

The more Daoist technique – advocated in the classic *Zhuangzi* – is called 'making all things equal.' This technique sidesteps attempts to fix the filters within us, and instead has us deliberately focus on the outside world, and to see all things equally, without evaluation. At its extreme, we have the sage Zhuangzi waking from a meditative dream. He then utters the famous line, "I was not sure whether it was I, Zhuangzi, dreaming I was a butterfly – or whether I was a butterfly dreaming I was Zhuangzi."

Several modern techniques have combined the cognitive and Daoist approaches – for example Dialectical Behaviour Therapy. This therapy includes a practice of 'radical acceptance' that is similar to the practice of the Daoist's 'making all things equal.' It was developed by Marsha Linehan, Emeritus Professor of Psychology at the University of Washington, who also taught Zen Buddhism.

Third, **declutter and simplify your life**. Sometimes we reach a stage where we have accumulated so many interests and obligations that we lack the time for true clarity regarding the most important ones.

There are several ways to declutter radically. First, just eliminate stuff. As Seneca said, "We are not given a short life – it's just that we fritter so much of it away. We have a long life, and there'd be plenty of time to achieve great things if we spend our time wisely ... We are not allotted a short life, but we make it so."[43] So, audit how you spend your time, and retain only those commitments for which you have a true passion, and/or where you have a unique ability to help the world in ways that you consider important. Delegate other activities completely, reduce your involvement, and say 'no' more often. Seneca allegedly created a baseline for simplicity – spending one day every week living as simply as possible, in dress, food, thought and activity.

Second, you can chunk activities so you are focusing on just one thing at a time. Multitasking is now considered highly inefficient;[44] it is certainly the enemy of *pu* simplicity. So, chunk activities into meaningful blocks. For example, we can end up reminding ourselves every day or week to do things such as professional networking; instead, chunk fragmented efforts on this type of task into a single monthly or quarterly time slot where you can afford to give it focused attention.

Finally, figure out the personal productivity system that works best for you in keeping organized. As David Allen, bestselling author of *Getting Things Done,* asserts, "To free your brain's storage capacity, you just need to find a system that you trust more than you trust your memory." What is your version of that system?

---

43  Seneca, *De Brevitate Vitae*, section 1.1. [Author's translation].

44  Shellenbarger, "Multitasking Makes You Stupid."

Decluttering your life at the macro- and micro-levels will foster *pu* simplicity, and allow you the freedom to fly – as illustrated in the next chapter.

## THE MAXIMS AND STORIES

These themes are explored in more detail in the following three chapters. *Fasting the Heart-Mind* illustrates meditative techniques. *The Frog in the Dilapidated Well* examines alternative perspectives, and *Cart South, Track North* illustrates an interesting example of confirmation bias.

As you read these stories, it is useful to ask yourself:

- Which prejudices (perhaps masquerading as knowledge, experience, expertise, etc.) could I live without, for a day?
- What situations do I see, with hindsight, that I could have addressed more simply than I did?
- How could I use *pu* to stimulate my own creativity or that of a team?

After reading the stories, you might decide you want to develop your own *pu* simplicity further. If so, use the template following each story to help you plan your development.

# 心 齋

xin zhai

# 10. FASTING THE HEART-MIND

Perceiving clearly
to lift life's burdens

Liezi had Old Shang as a teacher and Po Kao Tzu as a friend. When he had learned everything from these two about gaining clarity of perception, Liezi returned home – riding on the wind.

Yin-Cheng heard of this and went to see him, hoping to learn his secret arts. Several times he asked for the magic formula of clear perception, but Liezi rejected him each time. Dissatisfied, Yin-Cheng took his leave.

But, still driven by the same desire, after a few months he returned. Liezi asked him, "Why did you leave, and why have you returned?" Yin-Cheng replied, "You rejected all my polite requests, so I took a dislike to you and left. Now that my resentment has died down, I have returned!" Liezi said, "I thought you were smarter than that; what got into you? Sit down, and I will tell you what I learned from my Master.

"After I had served him, and enjoyed the friendship of Po Kao, for three years my mind eventually did not venture to reflect on right and wrong, and my lips did not venture to speak of benefit and harm. Then, at last, my Master gave me a glance.

"At the end of five years, a change had taken place; my mind was able to reflect on right and wrong again, and my lips were able to speak of benefit and harm. Then, for the first time, my Master relaxed his expression and smiled.

"After seven years, I could let my mind reflect on what it wanted to, but it no longer occupied itself with right and wrong, and I let my lips say what they wanted, but they no longer spoke of advantage and disadvantage. Then, at last, my Master led me in to sit on the mat beside him.

"After nine years of effort, I finally lost all notion of yes and no, of advantage and disadvantage, of the superiority of my Master and the friendship of my fellow student. There was no distinction between eye and ear, ear and nose, nose and mouth: all were the same. I had no idea what my body was resting on, nor where my feet were treading. Finally, I drifted at the whim of the wind, toward the east, toward the west, in all directions, like a dead leaf carried away, without realizing whether the wind was riding me, or whether I was riding the wind.

"This is what I had to go through in order to reach fulfilment. And you, who have only just entered a Master's house, who are still so impatient and angry; you whose earth must still support your coarse and heavy body, you claim to rise on the wind in the void?"

Yin-Cheng withdrew, not daring to answer.

———————

In this story from *Liezi*, section 2.3, we hear how the Daoist sage casts off the weight of the world. He became so light that he could ride the wind. After years of training, his body and mind, he let go of feelings of right and wrong, and integrated himself fully with the cosmos.

This story is clearly a metaphor. But somehow it works. We can identify with the feeling of being 'burdened' by events. We know deep down that this burden is created by our reaction to the events rather than the events themselves. We admit during moments of calmness that our self-burdening reactions are created by the clutter in our heart-minds. We recall that when we live more in acceptance of things, and co—operate with them, we can feel as light as a feather.

———————

The Daoist classics often refer to this process of decluttering as 'fasting the heart-mind.' It is also called 'sweeping the lodging house of the numinous [the spiritual/divine].'

Daoism's set of techniques for achieving this is called *neidan* – meaning 'inner alchemy.' In addition to meditation, these techniques include visualization, breath control, bodily postures and movements similar to tai chi and qigong. *Neidan* has several distinct goals. These goals include: to generally quiet extraneous thoughts uttered by the chattering monkeys of the mind; to identify and dissolve unhelpful aspects of desire and preconception; to expand consciousness and awareness; to become seamless with the environment and cosmos; and to become one with the Dao. Of course, the ultimate goal – as mentioned in the context of *The Ten Ox-Herding Pictures* in the prior chapter – is to then be able to carry this state into the living of life.

There are various types of meditation, and you may already have a preferred practice. The scientific evidence for the effectiveness of meditation is now great. One of the most-cited programmes using mindfulness meditation delivered reductions of 65% in 'total mood disturbance,' and 31% in 'symptoms of stress.'[45]

Specific Daoist practices for this type of self-development were based on the 3rd–4th century BCE text, *Neiye*. It is probably the oldest extant text on Chinese self-cultivation. Scholars believe it was transmitted orally before the text was written, as it is written in rhyme.

The *Neiye* describes techniques of meditation that are similar to many modern practices. The 'Fourfold Aligning,' for example, explains how to align the torso, limbs, vital energy and mind. This is similar to what we now call 'open awareness' meditation. In contrast, 'Maintaining the One,' in which the adept focuses on nothing but the way of the Dao, appears similar to modern 'focused attention' meditation.

The *Neiye* is couched in verses that have a practical beauty about them. For example:

> That mysterious vital energy within the mind:
> One moment it arrives, the next it departs.
> So fine, there is nothing within it;
> So vast, there is nothing outside it.
> We lose it
> Because of the harm caused by mental agitation.
> When the mind can hold on to tranquillity,
> The Way will become naturally stabilized.[46]

---

45 Speca, "A Randomized, Wait-List Controlled Clinical Trial: The Effect of a Mindfulness Meditation-Based Stress Reduction Program on Mood and Symptoms of Stress."

46 Roth, *Original Tao*, XXVI.

And ...

> Within the mind there is yet another mind.
> That mind within the mind: it is an awareness that
> precedes words.
> Only after there is awareness does it take shape;
> Only after it takes shape is there a word.
> Only after there is a word is it implemented;
> Only after it is implemented is there order.[47]

In addition to these meditation techniques, there are more directive techniques for developing your *pu* simplicity. These include cognitive behavioural therapy, mentioned in the prior chapter.

---

47  Roth, *Original Tao*, XIV.

**RECAP**

*Fasting the Heart-Mind* is a helpful reminder to develop *pu* simplicity in your life. You cannot develop 'flow' without it. There are various techniques to accomplish this, including meditation. As you reflect on how this fasting of your heart-mind can help your daily life, ask yourself three questions:

- **Is my current process for 'sweeping the lodging house' of your heart-mind sufficient?** You might meditate regularly or just when needed. You might use physical exercise instead or other activities such as playing music. Is it enough? Does it sweep your heart-mind or merely your mind?

- **Does this routine contribute to *pu* simplicity in my life?** How does it help you? How does it benefit you beyond merely during the time that you are meditating?

- **What other techniques might I find attractive?** Jot down your potential goals for further decluttering. Consider whether meditation, physical activity or other techniques such as visualization might help you.

# EXPLORING THE MAXIM

1.  Reflect: What aspects of this maxim resonated most with me?

    .

    .

    .

    .

    .

    .

2.  Consider: Where and how could this maxim help me right now?

    .

    .

    .

    .

    .

3.  Plan (optional): Define a relevant goal and how to get there *

    GOAL: *specific goal related to focus area: measurable, achievable*

    .

    REALITY: *where I am on achieving this goal: evidence from present / past*

    .

    .

    .

    OPTIONS: *3-4 different options to achieve my goal*

    .

    .

    .

    WAY FORWARD: *Chosen option: first step, by when, support needed*

    .

    .

    .

*See Chapter 17 for a worked example of using this GROW method.

# 井 底 之 蛙

jing di zhi wa

# 11. THE FROG IN THE DILAPIDATED WELL

Choosing constraints
that fit the purpose

'The Frog in the Dilapidated Well' is an ancient parable. The story first appeared in *Guanzi* – one of the earliest texts to influence and represent Daoism. It includes content from around 300 BCE, though the book is attributed to a much earlier minister of 7th century BCE, Guan Zhong.

The superficial meaning of the frog story is evident, but some of its deeper lessons are more subtle.

———————

The big black frog was not so big when he made his first and only transformation: from being a tadpole to becoming a young frog.

His siblings soon hopped away, and the frog became the master of his dilapidated well. He quickly learned the art of catching slugs, then worms, then spiders. He was happy to be at the top of the food chain, and proud to be master of the dilapidated well.

One day a sea turtle wandered by and peered into the well. The frog spotted him immediately, silhouetted against the circle of his Heaven high above him.

"Who are you?" asked the frog, "and what are you doing here?"

The turtle said that he lived in the ocean and had wandered inland to explore.

"You live in an ocean?" asked the frog. "What is an ocean? Is it as big as the well?"

The turtle laughed, saying it was much bigger than the well. Much, much bigger – and full of amazing food.

"You are a liar!" exclaimed the frog. "Nothing can be bigger than the well."

The affable turtle described the wonderful ocean. He invited the frog to visit him there, to see for himself.

"I know your tricks," said the frog after a moment's thought. "You just want to get me out of the well, so you can become its new master!"

In vain, the turtle tried one more time to persuade the frog; then he sighed and wandered off.

---

This parable has a deep resonance, and most people remember it after hearing it only once. That may be because the frog carries such strong imagery: 'frog' rates in the top 5% of the most imagery-rich four-letter words in English, according to several psycholinguistic databases.

The story appears in many cultures and across the globe. In Japan it appears as: i no uchi no kawazu (井の中の蛙). In Korea: u-mur an gae-gu-ri (우물 안 개구리). In India, Hindi has: kupamanduka-nyaya (कूपमण्डूक). In Sri Lanka: *kupa-manduka*. In Germany: ein Frosch in einem Brunnen sieht nur einen kleinen Horizont. In Russia: Лягушка, упавшая в колодец, не понимает море (uniquely in the Russian, the frog initially *falls into* the well ...). So, the meaning clearly resonates globally.

———————

The story has one obvious message, and at least two further subtle ones. They all relate to the idea of *pu* – achieving simplicity in perception.

The obvious message of this story is that **misplaced pride and will, walled-in ignorance, create the calamity of foregone opportunity.** The frog is like the child who presses her hands to her ears, shouting "La, La, La" rather than hearing the person speaking to her.

Interestingly, in *Guanzi*'s original version, the dilapidated well is not likened to an existing place at which we arrived and decided to inhabit. Rather, it is explicitly described as the circular surrounding wall of beliefs we have built based on false learning. We were not born in an existing dilapidated well, nor did we fall into it per the Russian expression. Instead, we imperceptibly built that well for ourselves ...

The second message is subtly different. It points, more broadly, to **the danger of refusing a call to adventure**. An opportunity arrived, but we failed to notice the herald, or decided to ignore her. We filtered things out.

The risks of refusing the call are obvious, and were set out in the earlier chapter, *Crouching Tiger, Hidden Dragon*. To requote Joseph Campbell: "Refusal of the summons converts the adventure into its negative. Walled in by boredom, hard work or 'culture,' the subject loses the power of significant affirmative action and becomes a victim to be saved."

We may respond to this warning by devising ventures, quests and escapades as an antidote to the dilapidated well.

We go exploring. But the way forward is not as simple as 'be adventurous.'

This leads us toward the third aspect of the story. The world is a place of endless opportunities. It's akin to the infinite library conceived by the writer Jorge Luis Borges. In the short story *The Library of Babel*, Borges paints the vision of a universe that is a vast library. It contains all possible 410-page books of a certain format. The books are housed in hexagonal rooms, and each side of each hexagon leads to a further room. You could get lost in there very easily, just as we can get lost in the real world of opportunities. The infinite library suggests a caveat. It hints at the tyranny of choice that might arise if you decide to have no well at all. It is the cautionary counterbalance to the more obvious reading of the frog story.

Some people choose consciously to live in a narrow well. It makes them feel secure. Others choose the opposite extreme – wandering the world footloose and calling it 'freedom.'

Thus, the third message of the story is a question. If we cannot be completely well-less, then we should **not be asking 'How do I get out of the well?', but rather 'What types of wells do I want to build for myself?'** We explore this question in later chapters, in which we explore choosing our purpose.

**RECAP**

*The Frog in the Dilapidated Well* highlights some of the risks of 'oversimplifying' our life. You can use it as a prompt to:

- Reflect on whether you have become too comfortable in your chosen well – by examining your routines, beliefs and prejudices.
- Consider whether more adventure would be advantageous.
- Examine what kind of boundaries you want to set for your 'simplifying' well.

# EXPLORING THE MAXIM

1. Reflect: What aspects of this maxim resonated most with me?

   .
   .
   .
   .
   .
   .

2. Consider: Where and how could this maxim help me right now?

   .
   .
   .
   .
   .

3. Plan (optional): Define a relevant goal and how to get there *

   GOAL: *specific goal related to focus area: measurable, achievable*

   .

   REALITY: *where I am on achieving this goal: evidence from present / past*

   .

   .

   .

   OPTIONS: *3-4 different options to achieve my goal*

   .

   .

   .

   WAY FORWARD: *Chosen option: first step, by when, support needed*

   .

   .

   .

*See Chapter 17 for a worked example of using this GROW method.

# 南 辕 北 辙

nan yuan bei zhe

# 12. CART SOUTH, TRACK NORTH

Dodging biases
to make better decisions

Near the end of the Warring States period (475–221 BCE), the state of Wei was in decline. Yet the king of Wei still wanted to invade the nearby state of Zhao, because it had been weakened by earthquake and famine.

The king's chief minister, Ji Liang, was on a mission abroad. But when he learned of the king's intent, he hurried home to dissuade the king. "If you want to win the trust of the world," said Ji Liang, "so that you can build your prestige and finally achieve your goals, you will not be able to do that by bullying the weak. Building prestige and bullying the weak are in opposite directions." The king was not convinced.

Racking his brain, Ji Liang continued, "As I returned home today, I met a traveller being driven in a carriage on the Taihang Road. He told me that he was going to the state of Chu. The state of Chu is in the South – but he was going North.

"So I asked him why he was going North, but the traveller replied, 'It doesn't matter, my horses are strong, we can manage it.'

"I persisted: 'However strong the horses are, you won't reach Chu that way.' But the man was insistent. 'I have plenty of money and rations! And I think we saw a sign back there pointing this way.'

"I tried again, 'Even if you have a lot of money, you won't reach Chu that way ...' But the traveller was determined, 'It doesn't matter, my coachman is one of the best.'

"The faster his horses would run, the more money he would spend on the road. And the better the coachman was at driving, the farther he would be from Chu."

Having seen the traveller's blinkered thinking, the king now realized how blinkered his own thinking had become; he decided not to invade Zhao.

———————

This story, like the story of the frog in the well, shows the dangers of narrow thinking. It shows how irrational biases and prejudices can lock us into the execution of our plan – so much so that we lose sight of our true goal.

If we are to achieve *pu* simplicity on our journey with the Dao, we must somehow recognize and dissolve these biases. We must refurbish the warped and smudged mirror of our heart-mind.

Chapter 10 (*Fasting the Heart-Mind*), showed how meditation can be used as a general method of springcleaning. By quieting and re-orientating our heart-mind, we can emasculate some of our prejudices. But the rationalist reader may want an approach more targeted at specific cognitive issues.

**Cognitive biases.** Cognitive bias are cases in which human cognition consistently produces representations that are distorted compared to some aspect of objective reality.[48]

The breadth and depth of our cognitive biases – the ways in which the mind tries to fool the mind – are huge. The Wikipedia article on the topic currently lists more than 100 biases under 22 major headings! The list makes for entertaining reading. It took me four attempts merely to count the number of entries, as I kept being distracted by intriguing biases that I never realized I had.

For example, there is the Dunning-Kruger Effect, in which unskilled individuals are biased to overestimate their own abilities, while experts tend to underestimate their own abilities. Or the Hungry Judge Effect, in which sensory input about one's body can affect one's judgment about external circumstances. Parole Board judges, for example, are more lenient when they have eaten and rested.

If we try to tackle these biases directly, we face two challenges. The first challenge is clearly articulated by retired Cornell professor of psychology David Dunning. In *Self-Insight: Roadblocks and Detours on the Path to Knowing Thyself*, he illustrates how we may lack the skill or will to even see whether we have these biases.

The second challenge is that we find some of our biases useful. These biases are 'heuristics.' A heuristic is a rule of thumb that we have evolved in order to make our life easier. A simple example of a heuristic is 'when driving to work, turn left off High Street if the traffic is easy, otherwise go straight on.' As evolutionary psychologists point out: if a cognitive bias makes us fitter, it is not a design *flaw* – it is a design *feature*. When it comes to the complexities of

---

48 Haselton, "The Evolution of Cognitive Bias."

interacting with people, however, our heuristics and biases become much harder to pinpoint. And the pros and cons of dissolving such a bias are hard to assess reliably.

People who have recently been promoted often experience biases of this sort. Their magic formula of skills, heuristics and biases had worked well for them in their prior role. They assume they will work just as well in the new role. This is reinforced by the fact that in any new situation, with its extra stresses, most people rely on their tried-and -tested techniques. But the reality is expressed succinctly in the title of coach Marshall Goldsmith's book on personal transformation: *What Got You Here Won't Get You There*. But of course, fresh thinking based on wider perspectives, and with *pu* simplicity, will get you to a better place.

Relating back to the theories of Kahneman, mentioned several chapters earlier, these heuristics are things we have worked out rationally with our slow, deliberate thinking, then gradually bedded down into our faster, knee-jerk reactions. Regardless of rights or wrongs, our self-justification of these heuristics can impede progress on dissolving the biases.

**(Dis-)solutions that can help.** What are the rules of thumb that can help us at least notice our biases, and perhaps modify them? Of course, in doing this we are creating a heuristic to examine our heuristics. We should recognize that this is all rather non-Daoist in that it risks complexifying things. But perhaps we can allow a brief foray off the Daoist path.

Biases have been studied deeply in the medical world, because doctors' biases can prove fatal. Reviewing the research from that field suggests several steps we can take.[49]

---

49  Saposnik, "Cognitive Biases Associated with Medical Decisions." Chapman, "Physicians and Implicit Bias." See https://www.physicianspractice.com/view/avoiding-cognitive-biases-decision-making.

50  "Your Lying Mind." *The Atlantic Magazine*, September 2018 print edition.

1. **Remain self-aware.** Ideally, we would regularly take stock of our biases and spring-clean the heart-mind. That is easier said than done, but at least we can reflect, noting those situations in which a bias is most likely to creep into our decision-making.

2. **Pause.** Acting quickly allows us to overlook our potential biases. In important situations, it can help to press the pause button and take precautionary steps, such as the ones listed below.

3. **Reframe.** By addressing a problem from a novel viewpoint, you may be able to de-bias your approach. Two prime strategies for reframing are metacognition and problem restatement. Metacognition involves 'thinking about how you are thinking.' For example: Are you using the wrong tool to solve the problem – like trying to persuade people by using facts, when they might be more amenable to stories (or vice versa)? Reframing through 'problem restatement' starts with asking whether the problem you are trying to solve has been correctly stated. Is it indeed the right problem to be addressing at all?

4. **Forced consideration of alternatives.** This approach works on your emerging solutions, which may have been swerved by bias. Options include: ask one or more experts for an independent view; radically re-brainstorm the solution – e.g., by asking what if we did the opposite, and asking whether significantly more (or less) data would reveal a different solution.

That said, many scholars are dubious about how completely this process will work, especially when we are under stress. Kahneman himself notes that, unfortunately, it is just when we most need this sensible procedure of noticing when we might be acting with bias, that it is least likely to be applied.[50]

## COGNITIVE BEHAVIOURAL THERAPY

A different approach, which does work in cases where the heart-mind is distorted by phobias, anxiety and depression, is Cognitive Behavioural Therapy. I mentioned it in the introduction to this section on Principle 4 (Simplicity).

Cognitive Behavioural Therapy is one of the most successful psychological therapies. The UK's Royal College of Psychiatrists states that: "It is one of the most effective treatments for conditions where anxiety or depression is the main problem. It is the most effective psychological treatment for moderate and severe depression. It is as effective as antidepressants for many types of depression."[51] You can also use it to disarm other prejudices and preconceptions that cloud the *pu* simplicity of your heart-mind.

The therapy is most readily understood in a simple but effective version of the therapy called rational emotive behaviour therapy (REBT). It was developed in the 1960s and 1970s by cognitive psychologists Aaron Beck and Albert Ellis to help people deal with difficult situations. In *How to Make Yourself Happy and Remarkably Less Disturbable*, Ellis credits the Daoists' strenuous avoidance of categorization as having influenced his development of REBT.

REBT uses five steps, summarized in the acronym ABCDE and indicated in the chart below:

**THE REBT PROCESS**

A is for Activating event: you notice and identify the event that is causing you a problem – in this case, things that cause you to react in a pre-judged way rather than a *pu* simple way. For example, "when faced with uncertainties, my first inclination is to gather facts, Google possible answers and strategize solutions."

B is for Belief: you write down the belief that is triggered by the activating event ("I must always be seen to have the correct answer"; or "I don't want to expose myself to unknown uncertainty and risk").

C is for Consequence: you write down how your mood or behaviour has changed ("All that thinking and strategizing makes me feel stressed and I will take up smoking again. On a ten-point scale of happiness, I've gone from an eight down to 2").

D is for Dispute: at this focal juncture you use self-talk to dispute your belief. (Notice, crucially, that you are not disputing the adversity or trying to find reasons for it; you are disputing the beliefs that lead to the consequent emotional change.) The disputation uses four types of question, aimed at generating a more positive perspective on the situation:

1. Is there any evidence of the Belief, or indeed evidence to its contrary ("Do I really always have to be right? What are the costs in terms of time and effort of getting it perfect? Perhaps the downside risk is actually quite small?")?
2. Is there an alternative, more optimistic, explanation?
3. Are the implications truly as I have seen them, or is this an example of me awfulizing and catastrophizing? Is the Activating event or 'Adversity' really that bad, or is it just a minor issue?

51 Royal College of Psychiatrists. https://www.rcpsych.ac.uk/mental-health/treatments-and-wellbeing/cognitive-behavioural-therapy-(cbt) Retrieved 26 September 2022.

THE POWER OF THE DAO

The D also stands for Distracting (doing something else to take your mind off it for now) and Distancing (stepping back to have a better sense of perspective, as a prelude to Disputing now or later).

E stands for Energizing: you determine and acknowledge that you have moved up from, say, two to seven on the ten-point happiness scale.

In the parlance of psychology, this useful technique is an example of 'attributional retraining.'

---

**RECAP**

*Cart South, Track North* reminds us to be on the lookout for the biases and locked-on thinking that can prevent us seeing with *pu* simplicity and clarity. Recalling this maxim can prompt you to:

- Familiarize yourself with the types of bias to which we are all prone – through reading and through observation of yourself and others.
- List a few of your biases (ask a friend for help on this!) and discern their usefulness to you – for example, by weighing up the risks and benefits and of dissolving them.
- Experiment with living for a day without one of your biases. Use some of the techniques indicated, such as reframing, forced consideration of alternatives, and perhaps Cognitive Behavioural Therapy.

# EXPLORING THE MAXIM

1.  Reflect: What aspects of this maxim resonated most with me?

    .
    .
    .
    .
    .
    .

2.  Consider: Where and how could this maxim help me right now?

    .
    .
    .
    .
    .

3.  Plan (optional): Define a relevant goal and how to get there *

    GOAL: *specific goal related to focus area: measurable, achievable*

    .

    REALITY: *where I am on achieving this goal: evidence from present / past*

    .

    .

    .

    OPTIONS: *3-4 different options to achieve my goal*

    .

    .

    .

    WAY FORWARD: *Chosen option: first step, by when, support needed*

    .

    .

    .

*See Chapter 17 for a worked example of using this GROW method.

無為
*wuwei*

# PRINCIPLE 5

# *WUWEI*
## (EFFORTLESS ACTION)

FIND YOUR FLOW ...
TO CULTIVATE YOUR ENERGIES,
RATHER THAN SQUANDER THEM

*Wei* means action or effort, and *wu* means no. So, *wuwei* is often translated as 'no action,' 'effortless action' or 'unforced action.' Clearly, we are now getting close to the idea of flow, in which we enable something to happen, yet it seems to require no effort at all.

The Chinese characters for *wuwei* are 無為 – combining 'no' 無 with 'action' 為. The character for action, 為, derives from an earlier character showing a hand engaged in the challenging action of leading an elephant. That character became distorted, though the animal's four legs remain visible in the modern version of the character. ('No', 無, is an evolved form of an earlier character. It combined the action of many (卅) men (人) on a forest (林), causing its annihilation (凵).)

The Introduction offered some simple examples of *wuwei* from daily life – from the perfectly cracked egg to the perfectly cracked joke. Chapters 13-15 give more extended examples of *wuwei* in action. They show a virtuoso performance based on a near-magical 'knack,' including the story of a cook named Ding. A hundred generations of Daoists have come to love this story. It tells of the cook who could carve massive oxen with apparently no effort all.

The way of the Dao enables us to access this flow state – either in a task, or even to live in it continuously. If we manage, intuitively and habitually, to observe *yin-yang* (energies), *li* (patterns), *pu* (simplicity) and *ziran* (self-so-ness), and work with them, then we will find flow.

Two points of clarification are worth noting. Firstly, you might object that surely nothing can be 'done' with absolutely no effort whatsoever! To this perfectly reasonable observation, some scholars say that the concept of *wuwei* means to use our insights into the cosmos, so that we use 'no additional action beyond the minimum necessary.' This feels a rather unsatisfactory explanation, as it undermines the core concept of *wuwei*.

Scholars still duel over the precise meaning of the word, but in the 2008 *Encyclopedia of Taoism*, sinologist Livia Kohn defines it as "to do things the natural way, by not interfering with the patterns, rhythms and structures of nature, without imposing one's own intentions upon the organization of the world."

A similar view, and my own preferred one, is explained clearly by philosophy professor Steve Coutinho in *An Introduction to the Daoist Philosophies*. He suggests that we read the word *wei* as not simply 'action,' but rather as 'artifice.' *Wuwei* then becomes act 'without artifice' – i.e., act in a way that is uncontrived, natural, simple and authentically in tune with the cosmos. Many scholars agree with this crucial clarification. 'No artifice' implies having a heart-mind that is completely unprejudiced, which ties into the previous principle of *pu* simplicity.

Secondly, as with all Daoist principles, *wuwei* applies just as much to nature as to ourselves. We will see that natural processes also operate on the basis of minimal effort. In following nature in this respect, we start to understand verse 25 of *Daodejing*:

> Humanity follows the Earth.
> Earth follows Heaven.
> Heaven follows the Tao.
> The Tao follows only itself.

*Wuwei* is central to the Daoist way of living, and correlates in many ways with our modern idea of 'flow.' The cosmos also operates with *wuwei*, and we can achieve many benefits by cooperating our *wuwei* with its. The Daoist engages with the cosmos in the recognition that *wuwei* of the universe and of yourself are inexorably woven together.

———————

*Wuwei* is relevant for us in three places. First, there is the *wuwei* of engaging in a specific task; second, there is the extension to the *wuwei* of living life well; third, there is the *wuwei* in governing a state or institution.

**Task-specific *wuwei*** is what we manifest when we perform a task with a smoothness and ease that surprises us. It could be an easy task like washing the dishes or cooking a meal, or a more complex task like playing a winning game of chess. The Daoist literature offers many illustrations of this, some of which are presented in the following Chapters 13-15.

Below I offer a personal illustration based on walking and mountaineering. It comes from *The Call of the Mountains* – a book that recounts my journey across all 282 of Scotland's highest mountains, aka the Munros.

It is while climbing the mountain called Sgùrr Fhuaran that I have a mind-body-spirit experience of the deepest impact.

I have been trying as far as possible to *wuwei* myself up the perfect cone of this hill, the last Munro of the Five Sisters of Kintail. *Wuwei* requires making subtle changes to my walking technique so as to be as energy efficient as possible and, more importantly, to be at one with the hill and the path. The efficiency with which we hill-walk is certainly important: to climb all the Munros requires expending approximately half a million calories more than in normal living, so any savings is worth it. More importantly, this mindset of least effort helps you emerge more completely into the zone of *wuwei* and its principle of intimate engagement with your surroundings and environment.

I am using techniques I had learned in the Himalayas – perhaps the best place in the world to find insights into techniques for walking mountains. Porters there often carry loads of twice their own body weight, do so consuming relatively little energy, and routinely achieve speeds that can be 60% faster than an untrained walker. After my return from Nepal, I tried consciously to emulate their walking style – both as I had observed it, and as I had read about it. There have been relatively few rigorous studies of Nepali porters, but Professor Alberto Minetti of Milan University did conduct one – the results of which were published in the Proceedings of the Royal Society in 2006.

Combining the findings of Minetti and others with my own observations, I aim consciously to glide up the hill, to walk silently and smoothly;,specifically, to walk so that I make no sound of footfall, and so that my centre of gravity moves as smoothly and consistently in a straight line as possible. Moving your centre of gravity smoothly is more difficult than it sounds.

It requires some practice, since for each step it means: a) not wobbling side-to-side, b) not surging forwards and backwards, c) not bouncing upwards and downwards, d) not detouring your path sideways from as smooth a line as possible, e) avoiding large steps upwards or down-wards by taking a line that has half-steps if needed, f) not wasting energy in stumbling or misplacing your feet, while g) not slumping your posture. These instructions are phrased as negatives; the positive is: just glide.

Having practiced these techniques, they have grad-ually become more automatic in recent months. But it is on Sgùrr Fhuaran that I am able to forget the techniques completely; my body has become tuned and entrained.

And then, as if by magic, I start to feel the walking is easier.

After a further ten minutes, the walking feels com-pletely effortless – even though I am going uphill!

And ten minutes after that, I feel the path rising up to meet my boot and lift me .... Words flit in and out of my consciousness, eventually forming a type of mantra:

> *When the path springs up to meet your boot*
> *The hill will lift you on your route.*

The path really is lifting me up. I feel I am putting in no effort at all!

As a footnote, you can imagine my surprise at breakfast the next morning: I notice the bread basket on my host's table – inside which is a tea towel with the words GAELIC BLESSING written across its top. I part the rolls and read the expression – which I have never heard before, and which by some strange coincidence completely reflects and encapsulates yesterday's experience:

*May the road rise up to meet you.*

---

So, task-specific *wuwei* typically shows, in the words of Lee Yearley in his analysis of the *Zhuangzi* : "adaptive responses to external changes; gains in power and efficacy without additional effort; unification of the mental and the physical; generation and manifestation of tranquillity; and the sense of participation in a larger, more harmonious whole."[52] Task-specific *wuwei* is the basis of many of the so-called 'knack stories' presented in Daoist texts. It shares many characteristics with Mihaly Csikszentmihalyi's concept of 'flow,' which are: 1. Intense and focused concentration on the task at hand; 2. Merging of action and awareness; 3. Loss of reflective self-consciousness; 4. Sense of control or, perhaps more accurately, complete absence of anxiety; 5. Distorted sense of time; 6. Experience of activity as intrinsically rewarding (autotelic experience).[53]

**Wuwei in living life well.** This raises the crucial question of whether and how we can chunk up. From performing a task in *wuwei*, can we live a day in *wuwei*, then move from a day to a week, and from a week to a lifetime?

In the story of Ding the cook (Chapter 13), you will see that by observing task-specific *wuwei*, Lord Wen-Hui then says, "I have learned from the words of Cook Ding how to

---

52  Yearley, "Zhuangzi's Understanding of Skillfulness."

53  Csikszentmihalyi, *Flow.*

nurture life." Wen-Hui has seen how to take the specific and make it general.

I believe strongly that this is possible. In coaching hundreds of very successful people, I have seen many who are driven and determined ... but anxious and unhappy. Yet I have also seen many who achieve great things with minimal effort, and who seem at ease with the world and engaged with it. They may be a minority, but they do appear to be living *wuwei*. I am not alone in believing that this is possible. For example, Rudyard Kipling, in his famous poem *If*, extols the almost Daoist lines:

> If you can keep your head when all about you
> Are losing theirs and blaming it on you,
> If you can trust yourself when all men doubt you,
> But make allowance for their doubting too ...
> If you can meet with Triumph and Disaster
> And treat those two impostors just the same ...
> If you can talk with crowds and keep your virtue,
> Or walk with Kings — nor lose the common touch ...

There are only two obstacles to extending the practice of *wuwei* from tasks to a lifetime. The first is the set of constraints that, consciously or unconsciously, we impose on ourselves. The second is the lack of encouragement to see that this is indeed possible. Providing this encouragement is one of the main reasons for writing this book.

All the principles set out in this book contribute to achieving this goal. They are brought together and illustrated in the final two principles of *de* (potency) and *zhen-ren* (mastery).

**Wuwei in governing a state or institution** is really no more than an extension of the preceding point – living a life in *wuwei*. The Daoists did not speak with one voice on this topic. *Daodejing* emphasizes that leading by not interfering is the best way to govern. It sounds attractive to the modern liberal ear, though it is hard to imagine it working in its extreme form. Other Daoist texts are less concerned with governance, focusing more on personal development. Although this book focuses on personal development in general, you will see that some of the examples do apply specifically to leadership activities.

## BENEFITS AND YOUR DEVELOPMENT

By developing your ability to *wuwei*, you will live a life of greater flow and contentment. More specifically, you will be able to experience more joy, even in mundane activities like washing the dishes; find that you gravitate to activities that fit most naturally and authentically with your skills and inclinations; and husband your energies – expending them wisely, and replenishing them from your natural engagement with your environment.

To gain these benefits, steps for developing your *wuwei* include:

1. **Be naturally and fully 'present' in all situations.** Adopt a relaxed focus rather than an intense scrutiny. Avoid multitasking. Apply your growing comfort with the other Daoist principles we have covered – *yin-yang* (energies), *li* (patterns and principles), *ziran* (self-so-ness), and *pu* (simplicity) – to help you into *wuwei*. This might feel unfamiliar at first, but soon it can become habitual.

2. **Nudge yourself into *wuwei* using small experiments.** Start with tasks in which you have already glimpsed your *wuwei* in action. See whether you can *wuwei* more consistently in them. Then try *wuwei*-ing in other tasks where you feel there is little risk in replacing your

normal approach. Then consider trying to live in *wuwei* for a whole day. Continue to extend the time span of the experiment. The three stories in the following chapters can serve as inspiration.

3. **Pause and smell the roses.** At some point in your development of *wuwei*, pause to take stock. Ask: "Is this working for me?," "Where could I try it more, or less?" Reflect on when and how your friends and colleagues are – perhaps unconsciously – adopting a mode of *wuwei*. See whether there is anything you can learn or adopt from them.

## THE MAXIMS AND STORIES

These themes are explored in more detail in the next three chapters. *Eye Not Whole Ox* tells the most famous example of *wuwei* in a task-specific setting. *Pen Dance, Ink Sing* explores spontaneity in more detail. *Inch of Time Worth More Than Foot of Jade* explores how life purpose and *wuwei* can fit together.

As you read these stories, it is useful to ask yourself:

- When was I most recently in a flow state of *wuwei* and acting with *ziran* (natural self-so-ness)? How did it feel? What conditions got me into that state?
- When did I last feel that I was having to bring a sledge-hammer to a situation; how could I have been more in flow?
- Beyond aiming for flow in a specific task, how can I start to live my entire life in flow?

After reading the stories, you might decide you want to develop some aspect of your own *wuwei* effortless action. If so, use the template following each story to help you plan your development.

# 目 無 全 牛

me wu quan niu

# 13. EYE NOT WHOLE OX

Gaining *wuwei*
to act without effort

Cook Ding was cutting up an ox for his ruler Wen-Hui. Whenever he applied his hand, leaned forward with his shoulder, planted his foot, and employed the pressure of his knee, the sounds of ripping skin and slicing knife were all in regular cadence. Movements and sounds proceeded as in the dance of *The Mulberry Forest*.

The ruler said, "Ah! Admirable! That your art should have become so perfect!" Having finished his carving, the cook laid down his knife, and replied, "What your servant loves is the method of the Dao – it is something higher than any art.

"When I first began to cut up oxen, I saw nothing but the entire carcass. After three years I ceased to see it as a whole. Now I deal with it in a spirit-like manner, and do not look at it with my eyes. The use of my senses is discarded, and my spirit acts as it wills. Observing the natural lines, my knife slips through the great crevices and slides through the great cavities, taking advantage of the nooks and crannies thus presented. My art avoids the membranous ligatures, and much more the great bones."

He continued, "An ordinary cook changes his knife every month; a good cook changes his knife every year; but I have used this knife for 19 years. It has cut up several thousand oxen and yet by carving with art, its edge is as sharp as if it had just come from the whetstone.

"Consider the narrow gaps of the joints. The edge of the knife has no appreciable thickness; when that which is so thin enters where the interstices are, how easily it moves along! The blade has more than enough room to glide casually in. But whenever I come to a complicated joint, and see that there will be some difficulty, I proceed with caution. I do not allow my eyes to wander from the place, and I move my hand slowly. Then by a very slight movement of the knife, the part is quickly separated, and drops like a clod of earth to the ground. Standing up with the knife in my hand, I look all round, and in a leisurely manner, with an air of satisfaction, wipe it clean, and put it in its sheath."

"Excellent!" said the ruler Wen-Hui, "I have heard the words of my cook, and learned from them the art of living."

––––––––––––––

This is a further tale from the classic *Zhuangzi* (section 3.2). The story vividly portrays a person operating in what we now call a state of flow. Psychologist Mihaly Csikszentmihalyi coined the term 'flow' in the 1970s. When in flow, you have a pinpoint focus exclusively on what you are doing. You are completely absorbed and immersed in it. You do not notice time passing. If you pause for a moment to reflect, you feel energized enjoyment – perhaps even a transcendent joy.

The story and the phrase are fantastic examples of *wuwei*. Recall that *wei* means action or effort, and *wu* means no. Recall also that a superficial translation of *wuwei* is 'action without action,' or 'effortless action,'; the more useful translation is 'action without artifice.' The idiom 'Eye Not Whole Ox' derives from Ding's words, "I see the ox already dismembered at my feet, like clumps of soil scattered on the ground." It reflects a spontaneous and uncalculated awareness of the intended outcome.

*Wuwei* is sometimes misinterpreted as a passive 'just go with the flow.' But the carving cook shows that there is a definite purposefulness about the activity. Crucially, the performer is not attached to a *precise* outcome, nor *how* the outcome will be achieved, but she or he nevertheless does have a broadly conceived mission.

The cook is clearly acting in a very spontaneous way as he continues on his *wuwei*. This spontaneity links to the Principle of *ziran* (including acting in a natural, self-so, spontaneous way) that we addressed in Chapters 7-9. (As we have now addressed four principles in full, and a further one in part, you will notice more linkages between them. Please think of these relationships as reflecting the holistic nature of the Daoist way – rather than seeing the overlaps as frustrating repetitions.)

———————

*Wuwei* and *ziran* are clearly keys – perhaps *the* keys – to living a happy and fulfilling life in flow. But how is this relevant for developing yourself and others? How does it relate to your role that may be as leader, coach or mentor? The key to learning these life-skills is clearly through mindful practice and awareness.

Gary Zukav offers an illustration of this in his book *The Dancing Wu Li Masters*, which won the 1980 US National

Book Award in the Science category.[54] This book explains the physics of relativity and quantum mechanics to the layperson, which were then relatively new to the public. But in the introduction, he reflects on how we teach and learn:

> The Wu Li Master dances with his student. The Wu Li Master does not teach, but the student learns ...

To illustrate this, he explains that the Wu Li Master does not talk about gravity until the student stands in awe as a petal falls to the ground, and does not speak of mathematics until the student muses that there must be a way to express a variety of observations simply. This approach demonstrates the power of *ziran* and *wuwei*, and can often be more effective than alternative approaches, such as directive learning by rote.

---

Pulling together all these ideas, the 'eye not whole ox' phrase suggests three ways for developing your *wuwei*.

Firstly, **dial up your spontaneous *ziran* (self-so-ness).** Recall from the introduction to Principle 3 (Self-so-ness) that Daoist spontaneity is not a whimsical knee-jerk action. While it is still a natural and potentially automatic action, nevertheless, it is one born of complete engagement with the Dao of a situation. It can be hard to find, but it's worth persevering.

Paradoxically, it can be especially hard to find spontaneous *ziran* if you are an expert in an activity, and have grooved your super-effective ways of doing things. It can be

---

54  Zukav, *The Dancing Wu Li Masters*. Zukav's 'Wu Li Master' is essentially an expert in the patterns of nature. A physicist or mathematician would be an example.

so tempting to just do your normal thing, rather than to absorb the unique and perhaps hidden Dao-ness of a new case. Sometimes you need to be nudged.

My own nudge came by accident. I had led a team to conduct an assessment of the leaders in a large organization. An executive arrived for his feedback a day early. I had only 15 minutes before my next back-to-back appointment. Our feedback sessions normally took at least an hour. And I had not prepared for this important meeting. But Jim had travelled for more than an hour to get to our offices and I did not want to let him down.

Jim managed a large sales force. He was underperforming because he was unwilling or unable to delegate. With no preparation and limited time available, I plunged in:

"So, Jim, what did you make of the report I sent you?"

"I liked the positive bits," he smiled, "but I'm not sure about under-delegating. I have weekly one-on-ones with each of my regional sales supervisors ..." Jim continued in defensive mode for several minutes.

With only ten minutes left for our conversation, I switched tack. "So, Jim, what would you like from our remaining ten minutes? How can I help you?"

Jim hesitated, then said that he realized delegation was a key skill for becoming a more senior leader. Did I have any tips? He admitted that he tended to be 'self-sufficient.'

"What kind of self-sufficient is that?" I asked.

Jim explained, adding that he had always prided himself in his self-sufficiency.

"Always?" I asked, "That's quite a strong statement. Any particular reasons for that?"

Jim thought for a moment. He tilted his head to one side. I could see a penny was dropping. Then he straightened up with what appeared to be a dawning realization. "Oh my God," he mumbled. "Now it all makes sense ...

My father died when I was ten years old, and my mother was not a strong woman. After my father died, I just *had* to be self-sufficient. And I haven't stopped acting that way for the last 30 years. I never ask anyone for help – just like my father didn't. I can see it all so clearly now." He stood up to leave, grasped my hand, and thanked me. I could tell that he was thanking me from the bottom of his heart.

Later that day I reflected. Normally, I would read the five-page report, noting further evidence to support what we had written. Then, I would summarize a few key points that I felt were important to get across clearly. I'd done it that way hundreds of times before. It always seemed to work. But I had been forced into a much more spontaneous approach, and with a gentle *wuwei* nudge Jim found an insight that he may not have found if I'd used my normal approach. Just 12 ½ minutes to evoke a great insight, versus an hour and a half to evoke some mediocre ones ... For a moment I had felt how a *Wu Li Master* probably dances.

If you are a leader of a team or organization, you need the skill of *ziran* (spontaneous self-so-ness). You will be confronted by unexpected situations requiring immediate action. There will be no time to use the muscle of planning, which you doubtless developed when you were a manager. Developing your confidence in using your *ziran* will be of immense help to you.

Second, try to **experiment actively with wuwei**. Consciously trying to be effortless might seem like a paradox. But it can be done.[55]

The story in the previous chapter gave an example of how you can get into *wuwei* mode through an activity as simple as walking across some Scottish mountains.

---

55  See Slingerland, *Trying Not to Try.*

If you are a leader, pick a forthcoming meeting, and see whether you can run it in *wuwei* mode. All great leaders conserve their energy, to save it for the unexpected disasters and opportunities they know will arrive. *Wuwei* is a powerful tool for conserving that energy. Moreover, you can't be a leader without having followers – and followers like the confidence implied by effortless action.

Third, **find inspiration from how other people operate in *wuwei*.** You really can start to *see wuwei* everywhere. Examples that might seem trivial or unintended can serve as a reminder to adopt it yourself. I notice, for example, that some of the garbage collectors in my local street swing the bins up into the collection lorry with apparently no effort. Their colleagues wrestle the bins, expending far more energy. Some customer service staff deal with customer complaints very naturally and spontaneously, while others struggle and make matters worse. By making a hobby out of noticing these things, you have a better chance of moving more into *wuwei* mode.

---

**RECAP**

Cook Ding's memorable story reminds us of how *wuwei* can be enjoyed everywhere. Recalling this maxim can prompt you to:

- Feel out the *ziran* (natural self-so-ness) in a situation – allowing you to operate along the natural grain and faultlines.
- Experiment, in everyday activities, with trying to *wuwei* – by using less forcefulness and more naturalness.
- Notice examples of *wuwei* in daily life, and the contrast when other people try to accomplish similar ends without using *wuwei*-ing.

# EXPLORING THE MAXIM

1. Reflect: What aspects of this maxim resonated most with me?

    .
    .
    .
    .
    .
    .

2. Consider: Where and how could this maxim help me right now?

    .
    .
    .
    .
    .

3. Plan (optional): Define a relevant goal and how to get there *

    GOAL: *specific goal related to focus area: measurable, achievable*

    .

    REALITY: *where I am on achieving this goal: evidence from present / past*

    .
    .
    .

    OPTIONS: *3-4 different options to achieve my goal*

    .
    .
    .

    WAY FORWARD: *Chosen option: first step, by when, support needed*

    .
    .
    .

*See Chapter 17 for a worked example of using this GROW method.

# 筆舞墨歌

Bi wu mo ge

# 14. PEN DANCE, INK SING

Using the knack of *wuwei*
to get it to 'flow'

This chapter's maxim, *Pen Dance, Ink Sing,* comes from a phrase in a 19th century Chinese novel.[56] This phrase gets to the heart of *wuwei* effortless action when applied to a creative task. The tool of agency (in this case the brush) is in motion in a lively, spirited and carefree way. This creates results that 'sing' – acting on multiple senses simultaneously and synaesthetically, and in *wuwei* for the performer and the world.

This chapter presents a selection of stories that demonstrate *wuwei* from slightly varying angles. They all illustrate the 'knack' of deft virtuoso action, taken from *Zhuangzi* and elsewhere.

---

56 Wen, *Heroic Tales of Sons and Daughters.*

## PAINTER ZHANG: 'RIGHT HEART-MIND, HAND RESPONDS'

Zhang, a famous painter in the Tang Dynasty, was renowned for his skill in painting pines and rocks. When he painted, he first held his breath as he sat quietly for a while. Then, when inspiration came, he would wield his brush as fast as lightning and paint the entire picture in a moment.

Bi Hong, another famous painter, had heard that Zhang painted pines with a unique technique. He asks Zhang to make a painting on the spot to enlighten him.

Zhang pauses for a few seconds, then takes up a brush in each hand, flicking them left and right. One brush is painting a branch, while the other is painting a dry stem on a separate canvas. The branch is budding in the spring dew; the withered stem sparkles majestically in the autumn frost. Every element has its own unique interest.

The onlookers applaud, especially as they notice that Zhang is using two bald brushes, with no hairs. And sometimes he uses no brushes at all! He merely uses his fingers to create the vivid landscapes of rocky mountains, flowing streams and knotted pines. When Zhang finishes painting, Bi Hong approaches Zhang to ask who his teacher was.

Zhang humbly replies, "I took nature as my teacher and observed everything in nature for a long time, so that everything grew in my heart-mind. When the heart-mind is right, the hand responds ..."[57]

Here, as in the preceding story of Ding the Cook, we see the hand acting spontaneously and in a skilled way. That is born from many years of the artist deeply observing the *li* patterns and principles of nature, and of sensing the *yin-yang* energy flows in the movements of himself and his implement. It reflects the *ziran* self-so-ness of how the ink and paper will

---

57  Adapted from Xin, *Historical Stories of Chinese Idioms* p 217.

inevitably respond to the varying pressure of brush and finger as they channel the essence of pine and rock. It reflects the *pu* simplicity in putting all the movements together.

## WHEELWRIGHT PHIEN – BEYOND WORDS

Duke Hwan was reading a book, and wheelwright Phien was making a wheel in the courtyard below.

Laying aside his hammer and chisel, Phien went up the steps and said, "I venture to ask Your Grace what words you are reading?"

The Duke said, "The words of the sages."

"Are those sages alive?" Phien continued.

"They are dead," was the reply.

"Then," said Phien, "what you, My Ruler, are reading are only the dregs and sediments of those old men."

"How should you, a wheelwright, have anything to say about the book which I am reading?" replied the Duke. "If you can explain yourself, very well; if you cannot, you shall die!"

The wheelwright replied, "Your servant will look at the thing from the point of view of his own art. In making a wheel, if I proceed gently, that is pleasant enough, but the workmanship is not strong. If I proceed violently, that is toilsome and the joinings do not fit. If the movements of my hand are neither too gentle nor too violent, the idea in my mind is realized.

"But I cannot explain how to do this by word of mouth; there is a knack in it. I cannot teach the knack to my son, nor can my son learn it from me.

"But these ancients are dead and gone in the next chapter, along with their unrecordable insights. So then what you are reading, My Ruler, are but the dregs and sediments of old men!"[58]

---

58  Legge, *Zhuangzi*. section 13.10.

Here we see themes of skilful craftsmanship echoed from the first story. To these are added a further Daoist theme: that we learn more by doing than by reading. This reflects the general idea that book learning can be too contrived and too far from life as it will be experienced. It also reflects the specific Daoist notion that books are full of words, and that words can intrinsically distort our view of the cosmos. We explored this notion in Principle 4 (Simplicity) on *pu*.

### THE FERRYMAN – NON-FEAR LIBERATES

Yen Yuan said to Confucius, "When I was crossing the gulf of Khang-shan, the ferryman handled the boat like a spirit. I asked him whether such management of a boat could be learned, and he replied, 'It may: good swimmers can learn it fairly easily. But divers, without ever having seen a boat, can manage it at once.' He did not directly answer me, Confucius – what did he mean?"

Confucius replied, "Good swimmers acquire the ability quickly – they forget the water and its dangers. Divers, even if they have never seen a boat can manage it at once. They look on the watery gulf as if it were a hillside. The upsetting of a boat is merely the sliding of a carriage down a hill. A diver has seen such upsettings and slidings backwards many times, and this has not seriously affected their minds. Wherever they go, they feel at ease when that happens.

"It's like in archery. He who is contending for a piece of earthenware tries with all his skill. If the prize is a buckle of brass, he shoots more timidly. But if the prize is an article of gold, he shoots as if he were blind. The skill of the archer is the same in all the cases; but in the two latter cases he becomes distracted and looks on the external prize as most important. All who attach importance to what is external become foolish in themselves."[59]

---

[59] Legge, *Zhuangzi*. section 19.4.

Here *Zhuangzi* gets to a psychological aspect of flow: what we nowadays call performance anxiety.

———————

These stories from the *Zhuangzi* and beyond suggest three themes that can inform our own development of *wuwei*.

**First: a focus on the doing rather than on the outcomes.** We live in a goal-oriented world, and it is tempting to prioritize the achievement of those goals. But Cook Ding, for example, is far more immersed in the process of slicing than in his final achievements. For example, he recognizes that there are some joints that will just not succumb to his knife and he seems unphased by that.

This echoes the research conducted by sports psychologists Burton and Weiss in their article *The Fundamental Goal Concept* published in *Advances in Sports Psychology*. They distinguish clearly between i) goals that are focused on the performance of a process, and ii) outcome goals.

In soccer, for example, process goals would be 'dribbling the football past a competitor' or 'making a long-distance pass to a teammate,' while outcome goals would be 'win the World Cup' or 'finish in the top four of the league.' Burton and Weiss found that process goals had several benefits for the athlete, or employee, over outcome goals. First, the performer has more control over how he or she progresses – and this encourages commitment and perseverance. Second, at crucial split-second moments such as actually striking the ball, a process goal is more likely to trigger the correct actions. And third, athletes who have established process goals are more likely to recover from setbacks in achieving those goals than athletes wedded only to 'winning the championship.'

The act of leading is, of course, a performance art. Followers rarely trust in monotone leaders who seem over planned. By periodically showing your passion and energy, you will engender trust and confidence. This was illustrated by the story of the pen dancing and ink singing. Of course, your messages need to be based on a vision and direction that is plausible and credible. But projecting this with dance/song will encourage your followers to trust you more – trusting your ability, but also your authenticity.

**Second, preventing the scheming heart-mind from suppressing our spontaneous faculties**, as scholar Wai Wai Chiu nicely puts it in Chapter 1 of *Skill and Mastery: Philosophical Stories from Zhuangzi*. He explains:

> The heart-mind of scheming may suppress a person's spontaneous faculty, that is, the spirit, not because of calculativeness per se, but because his or her attention is wholly bent to the outcomes of their action — or more precisely, the quantifiable social value of the product. In the process, one becomes a mere producer rather than a performer.

Or in Livia Kohn's words: "They get themselves – their personal concerns, emotions and mind – out of the way, allowing cosmic energy and spirit to flow and act through their subconscious mind."[60]

This theme, again, is supported by research. In an analysis of coping strategies used by US Olympic wrestlers, for example, 'thought-control strategies' were used by 80% of the wrestlers.[61] These included consciously blocking out distractions; explicitly putting things in perspective;

60 Kohn, *Zhuangzi: Text and Context*, chapter 20: "Skillful Spontaneity."
61 Gould, "Coping Strategies Used by U.S. Olympic Wrestlers." 83–93.
62 See Charness, et al. eds, *The Cambridge Handbook of Expertise and Expert Performance*.

using positive thinking, affirmations and coping thoughts such as 'using adversity as an experience,' and prayer. Other strategies, less focused on containing the heart-mind, were used half as often.

**Third, of course, is extensive practice.** Most of *Zhuang-zi*'s characters mention it. Malcolm Gladwell made famous the assertion that 10,000 hours of deliberate practice are needed to become a master in one's domain. Gladwell drew on the much broader discipline of expert performance, as researched by K. Anders Ericsson and others.[62]

Interestingly, the value of all this practice appears to go far beyond merely fine-tuning the cognition, dexterity and acuity required for the 'knack.' It likely has a cumulative effect on reducing the stressfulness of new situations in which performance is required. This reduction in performance anxiety, in turn, reduces the need for the heart-mind to set up a defensive scheme.

---

**RECAP**

Three further 'knack' stories illustrate *wuwei* in action, and we start to see the links to other principles we have examined. Recalling these stories can prompt you to develop your *wuwei* based on:

- Noticing the energy flows (*yin-yang*), the patterns (*li*) and the self-so-ness (*ziran*) of the circumstances in which you find yourself ...
- ... then absorbing these influences in a personally natural (*ziran*) and bias-free (*pu*) way ...
- ... and thus intuitively acting with minimal effort (*wuwei*).

# EXPLORING THE MAXIM

**1.** Reflect: What aspects of this maxim resonated most with me?

 

**2.** Consider: Where and how could this maxim help me right now?

 

**3.** Plan (optional): Define a relevant goal and how to get there *

GOAL: *specific goal related to focus area: measurable, achievable*

REALITY: *where I am on achieving this goal: evidence from present / past*

OPTIONS: *3-4 different options to achieve my goal*

WAY FORWARD: *Chosen option: first step, by when, support needed*

*See Chapter 17 for a worked example of using this GROW method.

# 寸 之 陰, 尺 之 璧

cen zhi yin, chi zhi bi

# 15. INCH OF TIME WORTH MORE THAN FOOT OF JADE

Focusing *wuwei*
to gain fulfilment

This final chapter on *wuwei* is about focus. Here we get to a crucial question: how are we to spend our invaluable time,if we are to live a contented and fulfilled life? So this chapter is about how we spend our time. It is about how we can invest it in the right areas, effectively – so that we can do our *wuwei*-ing in areas that are most relevant for us. This will also help us with our *de* (potency) that we cover in the next chapter.

The chapter is inspired by the *chengyu*:

> "An inch of time is worth more than a foot of jade.
> Time is difficult to gain but it's easy to lose."[63]

---

63  This advice comes from the classical Daoist text Huainanzi section 1, Paragraph 11.

I love this saying, because it invites us to compare something understandable (a foot of jade), with something less comprehensible and certainly different in quality (an inch of time). It gets you thinking – what is a foot of time, anyway?

This maxim goes beyond the simple equation 'time is money,' as coined by Benjamin Franklin in a 1748 essay. That equation is an alluring concept, particularly for people who are paid by the hour. Work more hours and you can earn more money. Work more overtime and you'll get richer. It is a simple formula. It is addictive. But it tempts us on to a perpetual hamster wheel.

Our maxim also goes beyond the mere lamentation that life is finite. Classical art is filled with images of *memento mori* – reminders of our eventual death. Salvador Dali's famous melting clocks, portrayed in his painting *The Persistence of Memory*, can be read as pointing to this brutal observation. Marlowe, in his *Dr Faustus,* has Faustus plead *O lente, lente, currite noctis equi!* (O slowly, slowly, run ye horses of the night!) so that he may delay giving his soul to the Devil as he had promised in his pact. But these are mere wishes to extend life.[64]

Our phrase also runs deeper than the quest for pure merrymaking, as in: 'eat, drink and be merry – for tomorrow we die.' That line of thinking was a favourite of Epictetus, one of the three early Stoics. It also found its way into the Bible.

We get closer to the heart of the matter through a Japanese Zen story. It appears in *Shasekishū*, a five-volume collection of Buddhist parables. It was written by the Japanese monk Mujū in 1283 and is based on the original Chinese phrase of 'an inch of time is worth more than a foot of jade':

64 *Dr Faustus* Act V, Sc 2.

> A nobleman once complained to Takuan, the great Zen
> Master, that his days at the office had become very
> tedious. He asked how he might better pass the time.
> Takuan wrote eight Chinese characters for the man:
> Not twice this day
> Inch time foot gem.
> In other words, this day will not come again. Each minute
> is worth a priceless gem.

This suggests that not only should we spend our time on the right things. It also hints that we do well to find satisfaction, and even beauty, in mundane things.

So, again, we get to a crucial question: how do we figure out where to spend our invaluable time, if we are to live a contented and fulfilled life in *ziran* and *wuwei*? Are there any techniques that can help us?

From reflecting on three decades of coaching people who have been talented, successful and largely fulfilled, I have recognized three steps. These steps are generic, but can help each of us find our own unique answers to the question.

———————

**First, rigorously take stock of which activities bring you true contentment and fulfilment in life** and spend time on them – not on activities that only bring you fleeting happiness or momentary joy (those benefits will arise naturally from living in contentment and fulfilment).

There are many techniques for uncovering what these core activities are. Having your own preferred model or checklist will keep you mindful of the things that are of true value in the current era of your life. It will help you keep your actions aligned with them.

Several of these techniques relate to your current stage in life. Hinduism, for example, suggests that our life inevitably goes through four stages: Student; Householder; Retiree (aka advisor or contemplator); and Wandering Ascetic.[65] An Indian colleague recently shortened and simplified this to: "Learn, Earn, Return."

Psychologist Erik Erikson offers a contemporary version of this lifecycle. He suggests that we grow through stages in which we ideally find healthy solutions to seven key paradoxes. Stage 1, as an infant discovering the value of Trust over Mistrust. Subsequent stages are: 2: Autonomy versus. Shame and Doubt; 3: Initiative versus. Guilt; 4: Industry versus. Inferiority; 5: Identity versus. Confusion; 6: Intimacy versus. Isolation; 7, in older age: Generativity versus. Stagnation.[66] Identifying the factors most important in your current stage of life is often a good starting point.

Stephen Covey offers another valuable technique. He suggests, in *The 7 Habits of Highly Effective People*, that we distinguish between our Circle of Concern and our Circle of Influence. By applying this distinction rigorously, we can see what things we should spend our time on. The larger Circle of Concern is the extensive list of everything we are concerned about. These concerns could range from the weather, to natural disasters, to the economy. Most of us cannot control these things, and we should not invest too much time in thinking we can. In contrast, the Circle of Influence contains only those things that we can control or affect. In the overlap zone, where the Circles of Concern and Influence coincide, is the group of those things that are simultaneously important

---

65 The four *ashramas* are: Brahmacharya (student), Grihastha (householder), Vanaprastha (forest walker/forest dweller) and Sannyasa (renunciate).

66 See life stages in Erikson, *Psychological Issues*.

67 Seneca, *De Brevitate Vitae*. section 3.1 [Author's translation.]

to us and also directly controllable. These include our health; who we associate with; our sleep; how we respond to the uncontrollable; perhaps our life purpose. These are the things we should spend more time upon, to live in contented *ziran* and *wuwei*. It's a useful review to conduct periodically.

The Six Basic Human Needs, as set out by Tony Robbins, is a third model that can help us clarify our focus. These needs that we all have to a greater or lesser extent are Stability, Variety, Identity, Community, Growth and Contribution. Appendix 2 in this book presents them in more detail.

---

**Second, having confirmed your focus and goals, ramp up your effectiveness and efficiency in using time there wisely.** To again quote Seneca, the Roman Stoic statesman: "No one squanders their money. Yet we all squander the one thing of greatest value: our time."[67] With penetrating insight, he continues with an intriguing list of how we typically fritter away our invaluable time.

Personal effectiveness and efficiency can both help guard your time. Being effective is different from being efficient. Warren Bennis, a pioneer in the study of leadership, said, "The manager does things right, but the leader does the right thing." If we apply this to *self*-leadership, we can say that doing the right thing is *effectiveness*, and doing things right is *efficiency*. So, how do we gain these twin generators of extra time, so we have more of it to invest in our chosen areas of focus?

A well-proven model for *effectiveness* comes from the world of leadership. Successful leaders do not seem busy. They have time to return your phone call. They do not need to reschedule meetings. They have time to mentor people. These leaders have time because they use time effectively, and that is normally through excellent delegation.

In many years of helping large corporations select their next CEO, my colleagues and I came to realize that this is an important CEO skill. This is relevant for all of us: it is being able to deal with 'the tsunami of issues' that will hit their desk every day.

Part of the solution is to distinguish between the important issues and the less important ones, and consider attending only to the important ones. Most CEOs, and the rest of us, do that fairly naturally. But the great CEO asks an additional question: of all those important issues, which am I *uniquely* qualified to do? And which issues could be addressed by someone else? The CEO might be expert at a topic, but if someone else is *more* expert, then the CEO's *unique* ability to add value is low. That second question unlocks the true art of delegation, by using it to triage things off the agenda.

CEOs limit their heavy involvement to only the topics that are both important *and* where they can *uniquely* add value.

In contrast, even for things that are important, but where they have a lower *unique* ability to add value, they delegate ownership of the entire task and merely define a way to stay informed of the outcome.[68] (They might provide personal input and, crucially, make sure there is a process in place that is robust enough for the CEO to have confidence in the outcome.)

That might sound complicated on first reading, but it does work. It can also work at home, not just in the office. A 2021 study in the US found that 84% of women and 68% of men did household activities on an average day, spending about 2½ hours per day on them.[69] You can save some of this time by delegating. If you have the money, you can

---

68  For a more detailed explanation and examples, see: Landsberg, *The Tools of Leadership.*

69  US Bureau of Labour Statistics. 2021. AMERICAN TIME USE SURVEY — MAY TO DECEMBER 2019 AND 2020 RESULTS. USDL-21-1359. Released July 22, 2021 https://www.bls.gov/news.release/pdf/atus.pdf.

delegate the laundry or dog walking. Otherwise, you can delegate to your partner and your kids. You can delegate to your friends' kids too – a neighbour's son or daughter is probably happy to earn some pocket money to open the door when you throw that massive party. And we can delegate to technology too. It took the COVID-19 pandemic to nudge us into realizing that we had better things to do than traipse up and down the grocery aisles.

That was about *effectiveness*. Next comes *efficiency*. To live life more efficiently, so that you have more time for *wuwei*-ing, there are many books and courses to help you. I found David Allen's course *Getting Things Done* especially helpful, including his mantra that to free up your psychic RAM – your brain's available capacity – you just need a system that you trust more than you trust your memory.[70]

My favourite example regarding efficiency may sound trivial. But it can save you more than 24 hours in every year. This is simply to use the two minutes every morning and evening, when brushing your teeth, to do a mini workout. Sometimes you could do a wall-sit. Sometimes lift a weight with the hand that is not holding the electric tooth brush. Occasionally try a one-armed push up ...

———————

**'Randomizing periodically' is the third suggestion for focusing your time only with activities that bring contentment and fulfilment.** That might sound surprising, after the somewhat structured prior suggestions.

By 'randomize,' I mean periodically to shake up your routines radically. This ensures you are not stuck in a rut,

---

70  Allen, *Getting Things Done.*

and helps you notice new areas that could lead you to even greater fulfilment. Let me illustrate with an example from the world of algorithms.

Algorithms are everywhere and affect our lives every day. They can also teach us the value and power of randomizing. Google uses algorithms to answer your searches. Facebook uses algorithms to feed you advertisements. Uber uses algorithms to find you your nearest driver.

These algorithms all aim to optimize. They do this by guessing a first answer – e.g., an Uber driver who is located close to where you are. Then the algorithm tweaks things a bit to check out some neighbouring answers – drivers who are just a bit farther away but might get to you sooner. If the other answers are less optimal, then they go with the first answer. Otherwise, they take the best nearby answer, and then repeat the process: checking drivers near this new candidate, to see whether there is anyone who can get to you even sooner. They do this for, say, 100 times, then use the best answer they find.

This process is called a greedy algorithm, because it grabs the best solution in the general neighbourhood. It is extremely good at finding what is called a local optimum – the Uber driver *in your general neighbourhood* who can get to you quickest. But there is a problem – it may not find the best possible solution – called the *global* optimum. For example, there may be a driver farther away, whom the algorithm did not bother to check. Although he is farther away, he is on a motorway and can get to you sooner. The greedy algorithm will not find this driver, so it will not find the global optimum solution. But better algorithms throw in a bit of randomizing. They check out a few drivers who are *not* in the local neighbourhood, like the available Uber driver on the motorway. That does not guarantee finding the global optimum, but it does increase the chances.[71]

I labour this point only because most of us spend most of our time using greedy algorithms. We visit the same local café for our flat whites. We read the same old media sources. We hang out with the familiar friends. But, if we are to find the places where we can best express our *wuwei* and find our flow, we have to be at least a bit adventurous. We need to randomize periodically.

---

**RECAP**

*Inch of Time Worth More Than Foot of Jade* is a reminder to discern which situations to spend time in for lasting contentment and fulfilment. Knowing this allows you to concentrate your *wuwei*, and in the next chapter, radiate your potency (*de*), into the relevant arenas. This chapter offered several techniques to help you:

- Take rigorous stock of what brings you fulfilment.
- Focus – for effectiveness, as well as efficiency.
- Randomize!

---

71 For more on algorithms, see, for example, Gigerenzer, *Simple Heuristics That Make Us Smart*, and Christian, *Algorithms to Live By.*

# EXPLORING THE MAXIM

**1.** Reflect: What aspects of this maxim resonated most with me?

> .
>
> .
>
> .
>
> .
>
> .
>
> .

**2.** Consider: Where and how could this maxim help me right now?

> .
>
> .
>
> .
>
> .
>
> .

**3.** Plan (optional): Define a relevant goal and how to get there *

> GOAL: *specific goal related to focus area: measurable, achievable*
>
> .
>
> REALITY: *where I am on achieving this goal: evidence from present / past*
>
> .
>
> .
>
> .
>
> OPTIONS: *3-4 different options to achieve my goal*
>
> .
>
> .
>
> .
>
> WAY FORWARD:  *Chosen option: first step, by when, support needed*
>
> .
>
> .
>
> .

*See Chapter 17 for a worked example of using this GROW method.

NOTES

德

de

# PRINCIPLE 6

# *DE*
# (POTENCY)

## RADIATING YOUR POWER ...
## IN A WAY THAT FULFILS YOU

If you have adopted the five prior Daoist principles, you will now be living with more flow in your life. In considering the sixth principle, you can reflect how you can 'live the Dao' more comprehensively across your life, to find continuing fulfilment.

The Daoist word for this is *de*. *De* is the way that the Dao of the cosmos is manifest in you. It is also the way that you express yourself to the cosmos. Its crucial importance for the Daoist is signalled in the title of the core text: Laozi's *Dao de jing* (literally: 'Way potency book').

We gain an inkling of the meaning of *de* from the structure of its Chinese character 德. This combines the symbol for 'go,' 彳, with that for 'virtue,' 悳. And importantly, the character for virtue, 悳, combines 直 (straight, erect) with 心 (heart, mind, soul).

The *Hanyu Dazidian* (the standard reference for Chinese characters) lists 20 meanings for *de*, and academics continue to debate whether Daoism requires *de* to be ethically 'good,'

THE POWER OF THE DAO

i.e., to benefit the cosmos – or merely 'right,' i.e., to be in tune with the cosmos. Many of the common translations of *de* suggest an ethically positive intent. These translations use words such as virtue, morality, integrity. But Daoists don't agree with 'oughts' and imposed moral codes. So some scholars read *de* as neutral in terms of ethics. They offer readings such as: power, potency, virtuality, personal conduct.

Several contemporary writers describe *de* as the particular power or potency that is expressed in the way that you live.[72] This manifests in the way you radiate an inner source of power that creates magnetic or charismatic influence. All things considered, I use in this book the translation 'potency.'

So *de* at least means in harmony and in co—operation with your cosmos. More practically, *de* leads to influencing, and perhaps nurturing, all things in a way that applies the principles we have already explored (of *yin-yang, li, ziran, pu* and *wuwei*).

The Daoist's version of *de* potency is therefore very attractive to the free-thinking psyche of our modern age. The Daoist *de* is *not* lived by adhering to a set of commandments prescribed by a religion. It does *not* require living to rules prescribed by a state, nor even to standards prescribed by a society. It is, in that sense, somewhat anarchic. Daoist *de* requires just one thing that is simple in theory, albeit hard in practice: to co—operate authentically with the ecosystem within which you live.

As Alan Watts put it, "*De* is the realization or expression of the Dao in actual living, but this is not virtue in the sense of moral rectitude. It is rather as when we speak of the healing virtues of a plant, having the connotation of

---

72  E.g. Slingerland, "Effortless Action: the Chinese Spiritual Ideal of Wu-Wei."

power or even magic, when magic refers to wonderful and felicitous events that come about spontaneously."[73]

Distinguished sinologist Professor P. J. Ivanhoe clarifies the distinctiveness of the Daoist approach slightly differently. "Laozi (the Daoist) shared with Confucius the belief that those who possess *de* will attract others to them. But the attractive power of Laozi's sage differs in character from that of the Confucian. The Confucian draws people toward him through the power of his ethical excellence, which inspires similar behaviour and attitudes in others. He is like the Pole Star or the windforces above the people to which they submit or defer... Laozi's [Daoist] sage also draws people to him, moves them to submit or defer, and influences them to behave in certain ways. But he draws people toward him and wins their allegiance by placing himself below them, welcoming all and putting them at ease ... Since people naturally respond to the example of a morally good person, such a person need not employ force or any other form of coercion in order to rule. He rules through the power of ethical authority."[74]

The foundational Daoist texts hint at what *de* is, though never define it precisely. *Daodejing* verse 38, for example, makes the following distinctions:

> The highest good is not to seek to do good, but to allow yourself to become it.
> The ordinary person seeks to do good things, and finds that they cannot do them continually.
> ...

73  Watts, *Tao: The Watercourse Way.*

74  Ivanhoe, *Chinese Philosophy.*

The Master does not force virtue on others, thus she is able to accomplish her task.
The ordinary person who uses force, will find that they accomplish nothing.

...

The kind person acts from the heart, and accomplishes a multitude of things.
The righteous person acts out of pity, yet leaves many things undone.

Or in Ron Hogan's brilliant colloquial translation:

People with integrity don't even think about it.
That's how you can tell they have integrity.
Other people talk about how much integrity they have, when they really don't have much, if any.
Truly powerful people don't do anything, but they get the job done.
Other people are always busy doing something, but nothing ever gets done.[75]

*Zhuangzi* uses the word *de* nearly 200 times, and in various contexts. Its section 17.7 provides one pen portrait of the meaning of *de*:

He who knows the Dao is sure to be well acquainted with the principles of things. Acquainted with those principles, he is sure to understand how to regulate his conduct in all varying circumstances. Having that understanding, he will not allow things to injure himself.

---

75  Hogan, *Getting Right with Tao*, Verse 38.
76  Hogan, *Getting Right with Tao*, Verse 67.

Fire cannot burn him who is so perfect in virtue, nor water drown him; neither cold nor heat can affect him injuriously; neither bird nor beast can hurt him. This does not mean that he is indifferent to these things; it means that he discriminates between where he may safely rest and where he will be in peril; that he is tranquil equally in calamity and happiness; that he is careful what he avoids and what he approaches, so that nothing can injure him.

An important aspect of *de* is the Three Treasures, called *sanbao*. These are compassion, simplicity and modesty. These are sometimes translated, respectively, as love, frugality and humility. *Daodejing* promotes them in verse 67:

The three most important qualities in life are
compassion, or showing kindness and mercy to others,
moderation, or knowing what a thing is worth,
and modesty, or knowing your place in the world.

Courage stems from showing kindness and mercy
to others.
Generosity starts with knowing what a thing is worth.
True leadership begins with knowing your place in
the world.[76]

So, if you are a Daoist, important aspects of your *de* potency are whether and how you choose to manifest the Three Treasures of compassion/kindness, simplicity/frugality and humility/modesty.

---

If you think rigorously about whether you want to adopt the Daoist route to achieving flow, you will inevitably come upon a central issue. That is whether Daoism allows you to define any specific purpose to your life, beyond solely acting in accord with the Dao.

In the strictest readings of some Daoist texts, the only purpose for a pure Daoist is to live at one with the Dao. That is, to interact spontaneously with the situation at hand. But most of us who are edging toward this pure state do have additional purposes in life. Most of us have purposes such as being a great father, mother, sibling, colleague, boss, friend. Or less nobly: to make a fortune; to live in ultimate hedonism; or even to rob a bank. Daoism does not forbid these purposes. It merely says that, because everything is connected, we are likely to eventually reap what we sow. Even in this lifetime, you will develop either good karma or bad karma (to borrow the Hindu and Buddhist terminology) and be repaid accordingly.

Interestingly, the core classic *Daodejing* does hint at a purpose appropriate for the Daoist. The book illustrates all the principles we have covered so far using extensively the metaphor of water. One characteristic of water is that it nourishes all things. In verse 8, *Daodejing* summarizes the supreme virtue of water:

> The supreme good is like water, which benefits all of creation without trying to compete with it.

The widespread appeal of this personal mission to 'benefit all of creation' is echoed by Marshall Goldsmith, one of the world's most experienced coaches. In his 2022 book *The Earned Life* he notes:

When I have asked successful people to characterize
the fulfilment they get from pursuing an earned life,
the number one answer by far is some variation of
'helping people.' I regard these responses as confirmation
yet again (if any more were needed) of Peter Drucker's
piercing but generous insight about us. In stating that
'Our mission in life is to make a positive difference,' he
wasn't exhorting us to do the right thing; he was describing what is already there, what we already know about
ourselves. We most fully earn our life when we are of
service to others.

So, we may resist going so far as to have no purpose apart from
solely co—operating with the Dao. But at least aligning our *de*
potency with being a 'nourisher of all things' can still keep us
on the Daoist path. The stories in the following three chapters,
including *Ghost's Axe, God's Skill* bring these notions to life.

You may want to reflect on what your current *de* potency
is and how you express it. The Daoist is a 'systems thinker,'
with antennae naturally tuned to understanding the connected ecosystem that is our world, and to the dynamic
undercurrents that link its parts. Thus in expressing his or
her *de*, the Daoist will be aware of a special synergy. That is
the synergy to be gained by co—operating in harmony with
their ecosystem.

---

To summarize: *de* is the set of ways in which you habitually
engage with your environment and the people in it. It is
your coherent and cohesive set of characteristics that show
who you are. The magnetic attraction you radiate and the
inspiring example you set is based on authenticity and the
Three Treasures.

You do not 'push' people by, for example, appealing to values invented and promoted by societies or states, which are ephemeral rather than eternal. (And don't even think of contriving authenticity, since you will be found out. In the more recent words, again, of Rudyard Kipling's *If*, "Don't look too good, nor talk too wise."). Instead, the authentic factors that 'pull' people to you derive authority from manifesting the natural and eternal way in which the Dao works.

## BENEFITS AND YOUR DEVELOPMENT

By defining what *de* potency you aspire to, and by developing it, you will find a clearer and more authentic way to engage with others and your cosmos. More specifically, you will have a North Star to guide you daily in how you co—operate with your dynamic environment. You will improve your relation-ships with others. You will have a more positive effect on them, with the benefits that accrue, both to them and to you.

To gain these benefits, steps to develop your *de* include:

1. **Know your values.** According to the Oxford English Dictionary, values are 'principles or standards of behav-iour: one's judgment of what is important in life.' There are several ways to take stock of these values.

   The simplest route is to write a list of what you con-sider your values to be. Then check with people who know you well that the list appears accurate.

   Another technique is to first reflect on one or more inputs before you construct your list of values. These inputs could include how you have reacted to particularly enjoyable or particularly stressful situations in the past. They could include the values of role models whom you may try to emulate or a generic long list of possible values.

A third technique is to construct a profile using an online inventory. Frequently used, albeit with limited evidence of accuracy, is Values in Action: https://www.viacharacter.org/. It profiles 24 strengths organized into six classes of virtues: Wisdom, Humanity, Courage, Justice, Temperance, Curiosity.

Ensure your list of values reflects how you engage with the world or contribute to it. For example, if you note a value as 'joy,' this should reflect how you bring joy to other people – not merely that you try to create joy in your own life.

2. **Know your magic formula, aka your unique ability to add value.** Your *de* potency depends not only on your values, but on other aspects of your own magic, winning formula. What else can you bring to the party, in addition to your values? It could be a particular skill, or knowledge, or something as simple as a contagious winning smile that makes others feel happy. More likely, your contribution is based on some *combination* of these things, and that combination may be unique – something that you alone can bring.

Knowing these things will help you cultivate your *de* potency. It will also give you greater confidence in exploring the Daoist way, as you live its spontaneous and intuitive approach to life.

The three techniques for identifying your magic formula are generically the same as for the values section above: self-appraisal with input from others; informal evaluation against the external criteria of your role models or listed criteria; and more formal evaluation online or by an expert in your field.

3. **Draw a picture.** Good old Laozi, Zhuangzi and Liezi would probably turn in their graves if they saw all the ink that had been spilled in writing about Daoism.

Too many words! Instead of writing about your *de* potency, engage your right brain by drawing a picture of your *de*.

Take a flipchart or large piece of paper. Then sketch yourself (and presumably your immediate ecosystem). Visualize the *de* potency to which you aspire, and continue sketching the nature of your interaction with your cosmos.

As I type these words, I recall an example of this, which in retrospect was a very Daoist illustration. Workshop participants were drawing a vision of their life in retirement. One sketcher drew himself as a battery – including positive and negative terminals. These terminals were connected to his family, his friends, his work colleagues and his clients. He visualized his interactions with them literally as flows of energy between these parties, recognizing that he had to keep the battery charged somehow. He added flows of current that included different voltages and frequencies. As an engineer, he then added capacitors and transistors – which confused the rest of us in the workshop, but helped him fine-tune his intended *de* potency.

Although he did not identify them as such at the time, the battery terminals were clearly *yin* and *yang*; the energy flows corresponded to the Daoist *qi*, and the voltages, capacitors and transistors corresponded with *li* (patterns and principles). Taken together, they added up to a picture of his *de* potency.

# THE MAXIMS AND STORIES

These themes are explored in more detail in the following three chapters. *Peaches and Plums Everywhere* examines the impact of our *de* potency on other people. *Carp Leaps Dragon Gate* extends this to helping someone to transform themselves. *Ghost's Axe, God's Skill* takes a holistic view of your *de* potency.

As you read these stories, it is useful to ask yourself:
- How do my values relate to the notion of *de*?
- How do I 'nurture all things'?
- What are the most powerful examples of how my *de* potency has received good (or bad) karma as payback?

After reading the stories, you might decide you want to develop some aspect of your own *de* potency. If so, use the template following each story to help you plan your development.

# 桃 李 滿 天 下

tao li man tian xia

# 16. PEACHES AND PLUMS EVERYWHERE

'Nourishing all things'
to build attractive charisma

During the Warring States period of Chinese history (475–221 BCE), the state of Wei was reaching its zenith under its leader Wei Wenhou. Zizhi became an influential minister – advising Wei Wenhou and securing powerful positions for his favourites.

At length, Zizhi fell afoul of court intrigues and, threatened with execution, fled to a neighbouring state. There, Zizhi complained to his friend. "When I was a minister back in Wei, I promoted many people. I trained and promoted half of the guards at the palace, half of the court officials and half of the border guards. Now the guards in the palace use the king to put me in danger. The great court officials threaten me with the law, and the men at the border pursue me. So now I will give up on training anyone."

His friend smiled. "Peach and plum trees are planted in spring. In summer, you can enjoy the cool and rest in their shade; in autumn, you can also eat their delicious fruits. But if you plant devil's-thorn, not only can you not use its leaves to shade from the sun in the summer, but its thorns will prick you. In cultivating talent, just like planting trees, you must first choose good pupils."

Zizhi could not return home, as his life was in danger. So he stayed where he was and set up an academy. He planted a peach tree and plum tree at the gate. Zizhi would point to the two fruit trees saying to his students, "Study hard in the academy so that, like these two trees, you can thrive and bear fruit. Only with exceptional wisdom can you nurture others and make great contributions to the country."

Under Zizhi's supervision, the students went on to great success. Many became high officials. Later, as Zizhi travelled, he was surprised to find that that his students had copied his example. They gave his philosophy enduring legacy, for they planted their own peach and plum trees in their courts and residences.

————————

Those who teach and develop others, whether they are teachers or leaders, leave an enduring legacy. The phrase 'peaches and plums everywhere' reflects this legacy, because peaches and plums are powerful symbols of longevity in China. And the plum – since it flowers in winter – also symbolizes perseverance.

This story originates in Chapter 21 of *Han Shi Wai Zhuan*, written around 150 BCE,[77] and has been used for more than 2,000 years to highlight this legacy. Today, this phrase is heard on Teacher's Day in China (10 September), in which families honour tutors. Indeed, the word *taoli* – peaches and plums – has become the idiomatic word for 'student.'

---

77  Ying, *Han Shi Wai Zhuan*, Volume 7. Chapter 20. [Author's translation].

This story and phrase suggest an important consideration as you develop your *de* potency: if you embrace the Daoist idea of 'nourishing all things,' then how can you manifest this chapter's maxim in your life?

There are typically four main arenas in which you can deliver on this aspect of *de*. The most formal arena is **through formal coaching in your role at work**. In doing so, you can develop both the skill and the will of your 'coachee.' This could relate to developing a specific skill, such as serving customers better. Or you could help develop a colleague's trait, such as getting along more productively with colleagues, or you could contribute to the colleague's career development, for example, by encouraging them to adopt a higher aspiration.

The practice of coaching has developed substantially in recent decades. There are many guidebooks and other resources to help you. I find the GROW model – illustrated in Chapter 17 – to be the most widely applicable technique.

The second way to 'nourish the myriad things' (aka develop people) is **through mentoring colleagues and friends, at work, or beyond**. The UK's Chartered Institute of Personnel and Development defines mentoring as the long-term passing on of support, guidance and advice. In the workplace, this describes a relationship in which a typically more experienced colleague uses their greater knowledge and understanding of the work or workplace to support the development of a more junior or inexperienced member of staff. It's also a form of apprenticeship, whereby an inexperienced learner learns the 'tricks of the trade' from an experienced colleague, potentially backed up by training.[78]

---

78  CIPD, "Mentoring Factsheet."

David Clutterbuck, an expert on mentoring, suggests that mentoring involves primarily listening with empathy, sharing experience (usually mutually), professional friendship, developing insight through reflection, being a sounding board, and encouraging.[79]

Coaching and mentoring are clearly overlapping notions – at least in the nature of the relationship between mentor and mentee, which includes strong empathy, careful listening and asking great questions.

The third arena for developing your peaches and plums, often overlooked, is **through the way you give informal advice to friends, former colleagues and others in your network**. Undoubtedly, we offer this help when asked periodically by our closer acquaintances. But I encountered a role model who demonstrates how, if we choose to, we can have a phenomenally greater impact.

In coaching a large number of people at the same organization, I eventually heard from *more than a hundred* of my coachees how just one of their former colleagues was still mentoring them. Really? Was one person able to mentor more than a hundred people? I was sceptical that one person could have so much impact, especially since he held demanding roles as a busy captain of industry. I pressed for examples. But their responses confirmed it: "He seems to reach out to me just when I need it." "He's always very natural: the call is apparently just to see how I'm doing." "Always has the knack of asking just the one pertinent question." "If I don't immediately see a way forward, a few minutes of conversation can point me in the right direction." "In the last five years, he has changed the course of my life, even if he does not realize it." This businessman

---

79  Clutterbuck, *Everyone Needs a Mentor.*

somehow found a way to do all this mentoring, despite being on the boards of several large public companies and many nonprofit ones too.

Those who achieve this breadth of impact typically start from a mindset of friendship rather than of explicit mentorship. They reach out to people in a generally helpful way, with no specific agenda. They are aware that their conversation partner may request advice – but are equally aware that the 'mentee' may offer helpful information or introductions in return. These mentors also typically have an efficient system of some sort. A good start is to make a list of the 20–50 people you want to mentor. Some mentors then ask their assistant to arrange calls with all the mentees on the list 'at some point during the next 12 months.' Others take a less-structured approach, and scroll through the list when they are on an airplane or in an Uber, to prompt a call.

Hallmarks of success in this arena are to be informal yet proactive, to help create focus, to be concise yet memorable, and to have no preconceived agenda as you reach out to connect with your acquaintance.

Fourth, is the **role of pater- or mater-familias**. Since children are so quick to learn, the 'good' or 'bad' aspects of your *de* are quickly emulated or perhaps rejected.

In recent years, as I have coached many people who are approaching retirement, I have noticed that those people who 'nourish all things' accrue great payback. As they seek to build a portfolio of post-retirement roles, they find that their 'peaches and plums' are now the very people who are in a position to suggest them for exciting new roles. This is clearly a form of karma rather than mere serendipity. But of course, the Daoist would not spend years contriving to support only those people who might eventually help them in this way. It only works if done naturally and with spontaneity – with *ziran* and *wuwei*.

**RECAP**

*Peaches and Plums Everywhere* reminds us of one very powerful way in which we may choose to develop our *de* potency (as an integral part of living a life in flow). Indeed, many people use this developing of others as a foundation for their entire *de*. The maxim can prompt you to develop:

- **A colleague at work** – through coaching.
- **A deserving acquaintance** – through mentoring.
- **A person in your broader network** – by offering advice.
- **A family member** – e.g., through great parenting or sibling support.

# EXPLORING THE MAXIM

1.  Reflect: What aspects of this maxim resonated most with me?

    .
    .
    .
    .
    .
    .

2.  Consider: Where and how could this maxim help me right now?

    .
    .
    .
    .
    .

3.  Plan (optional): Define a relevant goal and how to get there *

    GOAL: *specific goal related to focus area: measurable, achievable*

    .

    REALITY: *where I am on achieving this goal: evidence from present / past*

    .
    .
    .

    OPTIONS: *3-4 different options to achieve my goal*

    .
    .
    .

    WAY FORWARD: *Chosen option: first step, by when, support needed*

    .
    .
    .

*See Chapter 17 for a worked example of using this GROW method.

# 鯉魚跳龍門

li yu tiao long men

# 17. CARP LEAPS DRAGON GATE

'Daring to be great'
as a basis for visionary coaching

Aeons ago, in the realm of the Middle Kingdom – now called China – floods ravaged the land. Villages were swept away. Rice fields were drowned. The people starved.

Yao and his son Yu, the great ancestors of the Chinese, laboured tirelessly to drain the waters by digging a vast network of channels. But they laboured in vain, because the great Yellow River was obstructed at a narrow point near a mountainous ridge.

At last Yu discovered this spot, wielded his mighty axe, and cut a chunk out of the ridge. The waters cascaded out, and drained the land. But this created a towering waterfall and downstream all was swept before it. This was bad news for the carp, since they were all washed out toward the sea.

When the carp protested about their fate, the powerful Jade Emperor reluctantly made a concession. He erected a Dragon Gate at the top of the waterfall. He promised that any carp that had the perseverance to swim upstream and leap over the gate would be transformed into a mighty dragon.

So, every year the carp competed to leap the Longmen (Dragon Gate) Waterfall. Those who succeeded were indeed transformed into dragons. They were free to roam the skies and to bestow, usually, good fortune on the people.

---

This story has been recounted to hundreds of generations of Chinese children. The idiom 'Carp Leaps Dragon Gate' is used to this day.

Across many Chinese dynasties, a successful career could be gained by passing through the gateway of the notoriously hard Civil Service exam. Those who succeeded were called carp that had leapt the Dragon Gate – especially if the examinees had come from humble origins. In common parlance, therefore, the phrase describes an endeavour that will lead to a person's radical transformation.

This story teaches the power of perseverance, but it has further nuances. If your *de* potency includes developing people, you can use this phrase and its associations as a motivational tool in coaching, because it has three powerful features.

Firstly, the phrase features a **visionary goal**. The phrase describes an amazing feat, and is expressed in a way that is visualizable and, therefore, visionary. Defining the dream outcome, or what business guru Jim Collins calls the Big Hairy Audacious Goal (BHAG), has an attractive and motivating power.[80] This is helpful for the person you might be coaching, or for yourself if you are self-coaching.

Secondly, this phrase graphically features the idea of **the narrow gateway that must be passed to reach the goal**. This test appears in many of the world's myths, and clearly

---

80 Collins, *Built to Last.*

resonates deeply within us. Examples abound, for example, of the bridge as narrow as a hair that must be crossed if we are to achieve our transformation. These bridges are as widespread as Islam's Bridge of As-Sirat, Zoroastrianism's Bridge of Chinvat and Norse mythology's Bridge of As-Gjallarbru. Even *The Lord of the Rings* has the perilous Bridge of Khazad-dûm. Christianity has the 'eye of the needle' instead of the bridge. This narrow gateway symbolizes the realities and constraints that must be considered *en route* to the transformation.

The third feature of the idiom is the **idea of radical transformation**. The change described in the story is not a mere tweak to one's identity. It is a more substantial change to one's entire life. Some people will never aspire to such a change, but others do. This transformation is akin to the 'phase change' in the natural world described earlier in this book – for example, when ice changes to water and then to steam.

So, how can you put this phrase into practice as you help people develop ... *en route* to confirming your *de* potency ... and hence increasing your chances of living in flow?

The GROW model has become probably the most widely used technique for successful coaching and self-development. It offers a useful scaffold for showing how to apply the Dragon Gate idiom. I developed this model in the 1990s with colleagues, and describe it in more detail in *The Tao of Coaching*.[81]

The model consists of four steps. You can use it either in a conversation to coach someone else, or as a way to sort out a challenge of your own. This is an iterative model.

---

81 https://en.wikipedia.org/wiki/GROW_model.

You don't aim for perfection first time through it. Your initial perspectives are just drafts, and you refine those drafts as you cycle through the sequence a second or third time.

1. **G is for Goal.** A clear goal, or set of goals, is always a crucial starting point when coaching. Goals create an initial focus. Sometimes the goal is to develop a skill, and sometimes the goal is much bigger. Often the biggest contribution that you can make as a leader, coach or mentor is not merely to help someone develop a skill or deal with a specific situation, but to more holistically help them set a big exciting goal, literally daring them to be great.

   As you develop yourself or someone else, the idiom of the Dragon Gate suggests questions. These can create self-reflection and suggest aspirations to brainstorm:

   • What kind of dragon do I want to become?
   • If I were to become this mighty dragon, how would I want to deploy my new powers?
   • Is this dragon vision a version of my ultimate BHAG? As Jim Collins explains, a BHAG has three characteristics: the goal reflects my unique attributes – something at which I can be the best in the world; it taps into my deep-seated passions; and it is sustainable – economically or in sustaining my continuing interest.[82]
   • Is this dragon vision strong enough to help me swim against the stream, and to help me leap the waterfall?
   • Are there animals other than a dragon I might prefer to become, metaphorically?
   • Instead of Dragon Gate, is there a different metaphor for the aspiration that would allow me to transform in a preferred way?

---

82  Collins, *Built to Last.*

At this stage, your goal does not need to be super-SMART (Specific, Measurable, Achievable, Realistic, Time-framed). Forcing it to be SMART may constrain you, but in subsequent iterations of the cycle you will want to make sure that your own version of leaping the Dragon Gate comes into clear focus.

2. **R is for Reality.** In this second stage, you take an unvarnished look at your current situation and how you got there. This is *before* diving into the specifics of *how* to achieve your leap.

   You discern what has brought you to set this goal, what similar goals you may have set or avoided before, and what may have helped you succeed or fail.

   You review feedback from yourself and others. You explore your priorities, motivations, values, habits, emotions and limiting beliefs. As in the previous stage, you are not looking for an encyclopaedic set of answers – rather, you are trying to find two or three aha! insights that relate to your goal.

   Using the Dragon Gate story as a metaphor, you might also ask:

   - Does this dragon vision conform with my core values?
   - Will this dragon vision satisfy my six Basic Human Needs as described briefly in Appendix 2: needs for stability, variety, identity, community, growth and contribution?[83]
   - In what way am I currently similar to the carp? How do I know that?
   - Have I previously tried to swim this journey? Why? Why not? What worked? What hampered me? What were the predators along the way?

---

83  See Appendix 2 for a brief outline of Tony Robbins' thinking.

- What skills and abilities (like a carp's fins, muscles and proprioception) might I need to leap the falls and reach my Dragon Gate?

3. **O is for Options.** In this stage, you identify *how* you will make your leap. You brainstorm with a partner or on your own. You can use well-known techniques of creativity such a mind-mapping, Lotus Blossom and guided imagery.

Using a metaphor often helps in this process. It helps you see the problem from a new angle, and thus allows you to access unusual but relevant options. You could ask, for example:

- Are there other rivers that I could simply swim up to reach my Dragon Gate, rather than taking the steeper route up the waterfall?
- Are there staging posts I could find – like scaling the rockface by making smaller jumps from one rock-pool to another?
- Are there role models – carp who became dragons – whose techniques I could copy?

Beyond the carp, you can explore the field of biomimicry to find helpful metaphors. Biomimicry is the study of how nature has solved a problem, to solve a similar problem in the human world. Examples include clinging seed pods that inspired Velcro, the aerodynamic beak of the kingfisher that inspired the Japanese bullet train, and the backbone of shells that inspired building structures.

Or you can use the technicalities of the carp's leap to deepen or extend the 'carp leaps' metaphor. These technicalities have been studied in detail.[84] You might use some of the findings in the following way:

- The carp times its soaring leap to be propelled by the best undulation of the vortex in the waterfall's plunge pool. So ... what would be the best timing for your leap to take advantage of the surrounding circumstances?
- The carp does not actually swim up the waterfall – it flies through the air. So ... are you bogged down in too conventional a route up your waterfall; might there be other methods you could use: flying up rather than swimming up?
- The carp first swims with its body in an S-shape, then catapults itself from a powerful C-shaped compression. So ... are there different manoeuvres you could make, for different parts of your own leap?
- In a more extreme example: the mouth of the Nopili rock-climbing goby has developed suckers in its mouth to help it scale the rock faces behind Hawaii's many waterfalls. The application of this idea is up to you!

4. **W is for Way forward.** This final stage of the GROW model focuses you on your immediate next steps, so the W also stands for 'Wrap-up' or 'Will-do,' as well as 'Way forward.' You choose an option and commit to implementing it within a timeframe that you specify. Useful questions include:
   - What are my next steps?
   - Whose help do I need?
   - What resources do I need?
   - Am I committed to this route?

---

84  McDonald, "Can Salmon Swim up a Waterfall after Leaping into It?" Osborne, "The Hydrodynamical Performance of Migratory Salmon."

Good luck on identifying your Dragon Gate and leaping it to become a dragon!

> **RECAP**
>
> *Carp Leaps Dragon Gate* is a powerful and graphic maxim to inspire your coaching of yourself or others on personal transformation. It can:
>
> - Dare you to be great by setting a high bar to leap over.
> - Provide an extended metaphor to use in the GROW approach to coaching.
> - Serve as a portal into other fruitful aspects of biomimicry.

# EXPLORING THE MAXIM

1.  Reflect: What aspects of this maxim resonated most with me?

    - 
    - 
    - 
    - 
    - 
    - 

2.  Consider: Where and how could this maxim help me right now?

    - 
    - 
    - 
    - 
    - 

3.  Plan (optional): Define a relevant goal and how to get there *

    GOAL: *specific goal related to focus area: measurable, achievable*

    - 

    REALITY: *where I am on achieving this goal: evidence from present / past*

    - 
    - 
    - 

    OPTIONS: *3-4 different options to achieve my goal*

    - 
    - 
    - 

    WAY FORWARD: *Chosen option: first step, by when, support needed*

    - 
    - 
    - 

*See Chapter 17 for a worked example of using this GROW method.

# 鬼斧神工

gui fu shen gong

# 18. GHOST'S AXE, GOD'S SKILL

Applying the seven principles
to achieve astonishing results

Qing, the woodcarver, carved a bell-stand. When it was completed, all who saw it were astonished, as if it were the work of spirits.

The Marquis of Lu went to see it and asked by what art he had succeeded in producing it. "Your subject is but a mechanic," was the reply. "What art should I be possessed of?

"... nevertheless," continued Qing, "there is one thing to mention. When your servant had undertaken to make the bell-stand, I did not want to waste any of my power. I felt it necessary to fast in order to compose my mind.

"After fasting for three days, I forgot about receiving any congratulations or reward from executing my task. After fasting five days, I did not presume to think of the condemnation or commendation that it would produce, or of the skill or lack of skill that it might display. At the end of the seven days, I had forgotten all about myself – my four limbs and my whole person.

"By this time the thought of your Grace's court, for which I was to make the thing, had passed away; everything that could divert my mind from exclusive devotion to the exercise of my skill had disappeared. Then I went into the forest, and looked at the natural forms of the trees. When I saw one of a perfect form, then the figure of the bell-stand rose up to my view, and I applied my hand to the work.

"Had I not met with such a tree, I could not have proceeded. But my Heaven-given faculty and the Heaven-given qualities of the wood demanded it. So it was my spirit that produced the bell-stand."

———————

This is a further story from *Zhuangzi*. Qing shows all the virtuoso skills that we saw in the story of Ding the Cook and the other 'knack' stories in previous chapters.

But this time the fruits of the labours are so impressive that they gave birth to the maxim, still used today, that the work was accomplished so uncannily well that it must have been performed by the axe of a ghost and the skill of a god.

This story shows Qing's *de* potency at work in a specific situation. We can readily see that Qing demonstrates all the principles we have so far explored. From *yin-yang* energies, through *li* (patterns and principles), *ziran* (self-so-ness), *pu* (simplicity) and *wuwei* (effortless action). Taken as a whole, we see how he radiates a powerful *de* potency as he lives the Dao throughout this episode. His oneness with the Dao is so anchored and authentic that he can even project the mildly anarchic attitude, familiar to Daoists, of telling the marquis that he had even forgotten about the marquis' court.

I chose this story as a helpful foundation as you consider your own *de* potency, for three reasons. First, the story underscores again an important dimension of potency:

potency as skill and ability in performance. Second, it sets a nice high bar to at least start working with: living life with such authentic effect that your life looks like the work of a ghost's axe and a god's skill. Third, this micro-story illustrates potency as intent or ethic: a dimension beyond just skill.

Accordingly, let's see how Daoism addresses the topic of *de* potency as intent or ethic.

**There are no prescriptions.** On the subject of how you ought to live your life, as mentioned in the chapter entitled *De* (potency), the guidance from the works of classical Daoists is limited to hints and descriptions – such as the metaphor of water, which finds its natural way and 'nourishes all things.' There's no getting around it: the Daoists offer general pointers – not specific prescriptions!

Jiyuan Yu, the Chinese moral philosopher noted for his work on virtue ethics, emphasizes that Daoism's description of what living with nature amounts to is very 'thin.'[85] There is no holy book or prescriptive list.

This is good news for some potential Daoists. The freethinker who wants to define their own way, without the constraints of creeds and protocols, will find this attractive. But others, who seek clear rules and protocols, may become frustrated, albeit they may cherry-pick and use those Daoist's principles that best suit their needs.

Let's hope you are a free thinker who made it through that pivotal issue and that you are still with us ... and want to review the hints and pointers that the classical Daoists provide for living holistically in their way.

**Daoism suggests a 'virtue ethic.'** To be clear where we are heading: if Daoism does provide hints to ethical behaviour, these constitute a type of 'virtue ethics.' Virtue ethics is

---

85  Yu, "Living with Nature: Stoicism and Daoism."

one of three alternative approaches to defining your ethics. It emphasizes virtues, or moral character. This contrasts with the other two approaches. 'Deontology' emphasizes duties or rules, and 'consequentialism' emphasizes the consequences of actions.

The Stanford Encyclopedia of Philosophy illustrates the distinctions: "Suppose it is obvious that someone in need should be helped. A utilitarian will point to the fact that the consequences of doing so should maximize wellbeing; a deontologist to the fact that, in doing so, the agent should be acting in accordance with a moral rule such as 'Do unto others as you would be done by'; and a virtue ethicist to the fact that helping the person would be charitable or benevolent."[86] The Daoist is in the last of these three groups, although it could be argued that the first category applies in a specific way, in terms of maximizing 'the benefit to the cosmos.'

**Water is the most powerful metaphor.** Many of the pointers toward what your *de* potency might look like are found in the classics of *Daodejing*, *Zhuangzi*, *Liezi* and *Neiye*. These pointers, many of which use the compelling metaphor of water, include:

1. Embracing differences. Water can flow anywhere. The Daoist can interact with anyone or anything.
2. Nourishing the myriad things. Water can foster the development of others.
3. Holding true to your values and principles. Constancy promotes potency; the Daoist does not need to curry favour, nor undermine their position by shifting their beliefs.
4. Containing desires. Living joyfully and insightfully means avoiding fixated desires for people and things.

---

86 Mason, "On Virtue Ethics."

5. Being willing not to hurry yourself and other people. Sometimes conditions require waiting for the timing of the cosmos to be propitious.

6. Recognizing one's place in the cosmos. Humility and modesty are more powerful and enduring than fanfare and bombast.

You can use these pointers to enrich your statement of *de* potency.

---

**RECAP**

It is clearly for each of us to find, evolve and live our own version of our *de* potency. Occasionally, this can be realized through a sudden enlightenment; usually it is developed through more extended development.

*Ghost's Axe, God's Skill* is a maxim that can help you to keep your aspirations high.

---

# EXPLORING THE MAXIM

**1.** Reflect: What aspects of this maxim resonated most with me?

- .
- .
- .
- .
- .
- .

**2.** Consider: Where and how could this maxim help me right now?

- .
- .
- .
- .

**3.** Plan (optional): Define a relevant goal and how to get there *

GOAL: *specific goal related to focus area: measurable, achievable*

- .

REALITY: *where I am on achieving this goal: evidence from present / past*

- .
- .
- .

OPTIONS: *3-4 different options to achieve my goal*

- .
- .
- .

WAY FORWARD: *Chosen option: first step, by when, support needed*

- .
- .
- .

*See Chapter 17 for a worked example of using this GROW method.

真人
zhenren

# PRINCIPLE 7

# ZHENREN
## (MASTERY)

ATTAIN INSIGHTFUL MASTERY ...
TO BE CONTENTED, LIVING IN FLOW

So, where does this journey along the Daoist way take us? In other words, what is it like to live in mastery of the principles of Daoism, and hence in masterful flow?

The goal of this book, as mentioned in the Introduction, is to offer powerful techniques, drawn from the well-spring of Daoism, that you can adopt to help you live a fulfilled and resilient life, in flow. Should you, however, wish to embrace the Daoist path more comprehensively, you may want to see what the holistic end-point looks like: *zhenren*.

A *zhenren* is a true, genuine, authentic person, often said to have cultivated perfection, transformed, and attained or 'realized' the Dao. When you reach this stage, you are a sage or master. You understand intuitively how your cosmos works. You act spontaneously in line with the six principles explored earlier in this book: *yin-yang* (energies), *li* (patterns), *pu* (simplicity), *ziran* (self-so-ness), *wuwei* (effortless action) and *de* (potency).

The Chinese characters for *zhenren* are 真人. These combine 真 true, genuine, and 人 person. In turn, 真 true, genuine comprises the components for 十 (ten, and by implication 'complete, perfect') and 具 (ability). So, a *zhenren* is a person who has become completely able to live the way of the Dao. You are true, genuine and authentic, not merely to your own values but also to the way the cosmos ticks. This mastery is not mastery over the world, nor mastery over other people, nor even mastery of a task. It is mastery over your Self, including the way the Dao lives in you and in your interactions. You might also end up with mastery over the world, people or a task – but that will be purely a by-product of your Daoist mastery of your Self. A strategy of contriving and scheming for success is unlikely to be sustainable long term.

If you delve deeper into Daoism, you will find various terms for people who have achieved this stage. The Chinese terminology and nuances evolved over time – at some point implying attributes of saints or even deities. I favour the term *zhenren*, because it implies being true to the way of the Dao without necessarily carrying religious overtones.

As a *zhenren*, you have no particular obligations, though you will naturally act in a Daoist way, and will probably be seen as helpful, generous and wise. This is in stark contrast to many other religions that threaten damnation or an endless cycle of rebirth if you do not act in a prescribed manner. In Daoism, your only penalty for not becoming a *zhenren* master is that you forgo some of the benefits of being a Daoist.

Although Daoism's underlying practices have endured for millennia, the nature of the world to which they relate has changed drastically. But the notion of *zhenren* is arguably even more relevant to us today than to the early Daoists. Our own cosmos is a more hectic, accelerating and globally connected world. And many of us work in offices in large teams where we are denied the opportunity of creating a personal, tangible masterpiece. By becoming a *zhenren* – or nearly so – we can find beauty in the mundane. We can be content without always optimizing and indeed over-optimizing. We can remain balanced when the unexpected strikes us, and alert to opportunities hidden within uncertainties. We can side-step ailments such as boredom, loneliness and depression. We will see that this idea relates to the familiar Western concept of self-actualization.

The key steps to becoming a *zhenren* include selecting a few of the practices highlighted in this book and turning them into habits (practice makes perfect); fusing the way of the Dao with other practices you have found helpful (Daoism has influenced other philosophies, religions and thinkers, and vice versa); and deepening your intuitive grasp of it (e.g., by teaching it to others). You may also want to explore the *neidan* (inner alchemy) of classical Daoism, which uses physical exercises, breath control and meditation.

This final chapter reviews two examples of what the classical Daoist texts say on the subject of mastery; reflects on how Daoist principles relate to flow and happiness; and presents two final brief stories that further illustrate aspects of Daoist mastery.

## THE DAOIST VIEW OF SAGE-HOOD OR MASTERY

The term *zhenren* has not been defined precisely by the Daoists – recall that they avoid labelling and categorizing things. But there are many descriptions that illustrate what the *zhenren* is. The following examples show that the *zhenren* is someone who comprehensively lives the core principles that we have covered earlier in this book, and is living in flow with the cosmos.

*Zhenren* is often translated as 'sage,' but I prefer the word 'master.' The definition of 'sage' in the Oxford English Dictionary includes terms like: wise, discreet, judicious, having the wisdom of experience, indicating profound wisdom. In common parlance, however, 'sage' has the connotation of 'elderly' and you do not need to be elderly to attain wisdom. I therefore prefer the term 'master,' which is less ageist.

Some of the Daoist texts that refer to *zhenren* consist of advice for rulers. But the Daoist way is applicable to everyone, and at the very least one can interpret 'ruler' as meaning 'ruler' of oneself. You clearly do not have to rule a country, nor even be a leader to be a *zhenren*. We can all live in mastery within our own ecosystems of family, workplace and social environment.

Descriptions of *zhenren* notably include the final verse of **Daodejing**:

> True words do not sound beautiful; beautiful sounding words are not true.
> Wise men don't need to debate; men who need to debate are not wise.
> Wise men are not scholars, and scholars are not wise.
> The Master desires no possessions.
> Since the things she does are for the people, she has more than she needs.
> The more she gives to others, the more she has for herself.
> The Tao of Heaven nourishes by not forcing.
> The Tao of the Wise person acts by not competing.

Here we see that the *zhenren* i) avoids contrived argumentation and compartmentalized thinking; ii) does not need to hoard or even possess 'things'; iii) recognizes that giving is getting; and iv) acts *wuwei* rather than by forcing things.

Though this verse appears in *Daodejing*'s second half, which focuses on advice for rulers, it is clear how we could choose to live this description in the governance of our lives more broadly.

The **Zhuangzi**, sections 6.2 and 6.3 offer:

> The zhenren of old ... did not seek to accomplish their ends like heroes ... Though they might succeed, they had no self-complacency. Being such, they could ascend the loftiest heights without fear...
>
> They did not dream when they slept, had no anxiety when they awoke, and did not care that their food should be pleasant ...
>
> Entrance into life occasioned them no joy; the exit from it awakened no resistance. Composedly they went and came. They did not forget what their beginning had been, and they did not inquire into what their end would be. They accepted their life and rejoiced in it; they forgot all fear of death ...
>
> Their minds were free from all thought; their demeanour was still and unmoved; their foreheads beamed simplicity.

Here we again see the emphasis on *wuwei*: of avoiding the struggle of overthinking; emphasis on avoiding excessive desire; and a reference to the somatic aspects of relaxed sleeping and breathing.

Later Daoism added strongly religious overtones to the notion of *zhenren*. The many Daoist schools that emerged after Laozi and Zhuangzi valorized the mystical aspects of Daoism, and emphasized the *zhenren*'s ability not merely to transcend the world and become the Dao, but also to display superhuman abilities. Please follow the links in the Further Reading if you wish to explore this transcendent theme in more detail.

To summarize: the highest stage of Daoist development is the *zhenren*. This is a true, genuine, authentic person, often said to have cultivated perfection, transformed, and attained or 'realized' the Dao. When you reach this stage, you are indeed a master. You grasp intuitively how your cosmos works and you act spontaneously in line with the six themes explored earlier: *yin-yang* (energies), *li* (patterns), *pu* (simplicity), *ziran* (natural self-so-ness), *wuwei* (effortless action) and *de* (potency). The term 'master' might sound grandiose, but refers to wisdom in any activity. We can all become masterly in our own domains.

## THE LINK TO FLOW

In our current age – with a pandemic, questionable government, economic rollercoasters, and radical climate change – our ability to access the calm yet focused, productive and happy state of flow has rarely been of greater value.

But the reader of rigorous mindset will ask: are these principles of Daoism both necessary and sufficient to achieve a state of flow at the micro level of *task*, and also at the macro level of *lifetime*?

Firstly, flow at the level of performing specific *tasks* has now been studied for decades. While the precise neuroscience of flow is still being researched, there is now a clear picture of the factors that contribute to it. These contributory factors are very similar to the principles of Daoism. My own reading of the evidence is, therefore, a qualified 'yes': the Daoist principles are indeed both necessary and sufficient for achieving in-task flow. My only qualification relates to the prevailing view that in-task flow can only be achieved when the degree of challenge matches the just-comfortable highest levels of the performer's skills. Here I believe that Daoist principles can allow in-task flow, regardless of the level of challenge. This is because the Daoist way builds ultimate levels of relaxed confidence and resilience, allowing the Daoist to approach *any* task, however challenging, with his or her best self.

Secondly, is the Daoist way necessary and/or sufficient for living your entire *life* in flow? I have concluded that, based on seeing the lives of the hundreds of people I have coached over the decades, this way is certainly sufficient. I also believe its principles are necessary (though you might follow them through a religion or philosophy of a different name).

Moreover, each one of the Daoist principles is valuable independently, in its own right. You can experiment by buying into just one or two principles, and then commit to the Daoist way more holistically if your experiments work for you.

## THE LINK TO HAPPINESS

Any code of conduct must offer joy and happiness if one is to be motivated to follow it. I have pointed to a few examples provided by Daoism: the joyful spontaneity of the artist as he painted with both hands at once; the contented virtuosity of the other craftsmen such as Ding the Cook and Qing the Woodcarver; and the abandon of Liezi as he rode the wind.

But casting your mind back over the seven principles I have offered, Daoism might on the surface appear dry and stoic. Steve Coutinho echoes this in his *An Introduction to Daoist Philosophies*. Commenting on the notion of not allowing your desires to get in your way, he says:

A common objection to this sort of [stoic/Daoist] ideal is that a life of emotional indifference is a diminished life. Is it not important to feel everything vividly, to live through every detail of our lives with passionate intensity? This objection rests on a misunderstanding. The person who cultivates a [stoic/Daoist] attitude is not cold and impassive, apathetic and emotionally dead. On the contrary, the ideal is precisely to live in fullest appreciation and joyful acceptance of every moment of one's life. Therefore, sages wander in the realm where things cannot escape, and all are preserved. They delight in early death; they delight in old age; they delight in the beginning; they delight in the end.[87]

This view is repeated in Sun Yiping's "On the Characteristics and Modern Relevance of the Taoist Concept of Happiness":

Desire is the desire to obtain something or to achieve a certain goal, which in itself is not good or bad, but if the unhealthy or unreasonable desire is too strong, resulting in consequences that directly affect their own or other people's survival, there will be the difference between good and evil, happiness and misfortune.[88]

Finally, as Alan Watts observed, though the Eastern and Western paths of self-development may have their differences, their endpoints bear striking similarities. He points out that Eastern philosophies are perfectly in accord with individuation (Jung), self-actualization (Maslow), functional autonomy (Allport) or creative selfhood (Adler).[89]

87 Coutinho, *An Introduction to Daoist Philosophies*, 70.
88 Sun, "On the Characteristics and Modern Relevance of the Taoist Concept of Happiness."
89 Watts, *Psychotherapy East and West*.

You may find it helpful to perceive your *de* potency and *zhenren* mastery, and the happiness and fulfilment that they bring, with the help of these Western lenses. The principles of Daoism offer practical steps to this common end.

## TWO CONCLUDING STORIES AND MAXIMS

I conclude with two of my favourite *chengyu* – those pithy Chinese expressions of four characters, which embody a whole story full of meaning. Both *chengyu* reflect an aspect of Daoist mastery.

### MORNING THREE, AFTERNOON FOUR
### (朝三暮四 – ZHAO SAN MU SI)

A keeper of monkeys was about to feed them their acorns.

"In the morning I'll give you three," he said, "and in the evening four."

The monkeys were furious and leapt about. "OK, I hear you," he said. "I'll give you four in the morning and three in the evening."

Now the monkeys leapt about in delight.

His two proposals were substantially the same; one made them angry, and the other made them pleased.

This sagely man understood the demands and denials, and was able to resolve the issue harmoniously. He saw both sides of the dispute and just went along with it.

———

This is a story from *Zhuangzi*, section 2.6. As Edward Slingerland observes:

> Monkeys served as symbols of wilful ignorance and cognitive rigidity, and here they are meant to represent the average person, sure of what he wants and doesn't want, with very full boats indeed. The way to handle monkeys – human or otherwise – is just to let them have their way, if there is no harm in it, rather than insisting on one's original plan. This is 'going along with things.'

The monkey trainer demonstrates, in a very simple way, many of the principles we have explored in this book. He is alert to the interplay between the *yang* emotionality of the monkeys and the *yin* potentiality of the nuts. He plays with the *li* patterns and principles of 'three then four' versus 'four then three.' He acts in the moment with *ziran* spontaneity and *pu* simplicity. Most strikingly, he solves the feeding problem with *wuwei* minimal effort – acting without force, and without lugging additional things or energy into the situation. We also see his *de* potency at work: he knows he has the power (he holds the nuts as his trump cards), but he nevertheless acts in an agreeable manner to the monkeys as he embraces their apparent concerns.

## FILE PESTLE CREATE NEEDLE
### (磨杵成針 – MO CHU CHENG ZHEN)

Xuanwu is revered by religious Daoists as one of their most powerful gods. Before his deification, at the age of 15, Prince Xuanwu ran away from home and settled deep in the forests of Wudang Mountain. He spent many years in contemplation there to purify his spirit.

One day he became disheartened because his efforts were yielding little progress. He gave up and decided to return home. As he traipsed down the hillside, he came to a well. There he saw an elderly lady hunched over a table. She was filing down a thick iron bar. Xuanwu asked what she was doing and she replied that she was sharpening the iron pestle into a needle.

"But that's surely too much hard work!" exclaimed the prince. "When I have sharpened the iron bar into a needle," replied the elderly lady, "The work will have come to its natural and spontaneous fruition." Xuanwu thought for a moment and was inspired by the effort and determination of this disguised deity. He recognized that while *wuwei* is artifice-less, it is not always effortless, and he returned to his work of inner alchemy, with eventual success …

The story signals the importance of perseverance on our journeys to mastery. I like it not because of the complexity of the message, but because its powerful imagery is so memorable. Once heard, the story is hard to forget. I find it pops up naturally as a reminder when my own perseverance starts to flag.

And that needle is a great reminder of the ubiquitous power of *yin-yang*. As highlighted in the Introduction, its sharp *yang* point would be useless without its empty *yin* eye.

---

Reflections that the notion of *zhenren* might trigger include:

- Is the concept of *zhenren* mastery an attractive one, which I wish to develop? Am I still persevering on my journey to attaining the Dao?
- What kind of magic do I work, or aspire to work, in my mastery?
- How does the notion of *zhenren* relate to my views on spirituality?

# SUMMARY AND CHECKLIST

The core principles and habits of Daoism help you deliver virtuoso performance and live in flow, fulfilment and resilience.

As our world becomes ever more complex and unpredictable, such a toolkit is becoming ever more valuable.

Daoism helps by offering pointers for how to see the world more clearly, and how to act with authentic spontaneity. This allows you to 'get out of your own way,' and to co—operate your flow of *qi* energy with that of your cosmos. You flow it wisely to your family, friends, teams and environment, and will likely receive its flow back to you in some way.

The principles of Daoism are based on a few underlying beliefs. These beliefs include: that the cosmos is a connected ecosystem; that change is continuous and pervasive; that we are better off working *with* the dynamics of our team, family or environment rather than going squarely against the cosmos; that self-development is a worthwhile venture; and that often we need to discard assumptions in order to see the world with greater clarity and simplicity.

Of the seven principles presented in this book, three are primarily about habitually noticing how we and the cosmos work (*yin-yang* energies, *li* patterns and *ziran* self-so-ness). Three others are more about how we choose to behave (*pu* simplicity, *wuwei* effortless action, and *de* potency). These allow us to access the final principle of *zhenren* (mastery). These principles lead to specific habits and benefits as summarized below.

1. *Yin* and *yang* represent energies and energy flows. *Yin* is the dark, receptive and least obvious side of things. *Yang* is the bright, forceful and often more evident side. *Yin* and *yang* arise mutually and in cycles. The habit associated with this principle is to discern the energy flows in a situation, and to be attuned with them, so you can better see opportunities and threats. To build this habit:

☐ Practice feeling the *yin* and *yang* in different situations.

☐ Sensitize your antennae to how *yin* may change into *yang* and back again, and notice the energy flows.

☐ Experiment consciously, and perhaps radically, with trying to act with more *yin* or more *yang*.

2. *Li* represents the patterns in ourselves and in our environment. By grounding yourself in the fundamental principles of your environment, rather than in transient factors, you get better at 'connecting the dots.' This helps you to more creative and robust solutions. The relevant habit is to recognize these patterns, so you can spot when and how to act. To build this habit:

☐ Take time to notice the patterns – both static and dynamic.

☐ Become T-shaped – deeply expert in certain areas, but informed by a perspective across others too.

☐ Accumulate a knowledge bank of patterns and principles most relevant to you.

3. **Ziran** represents the natural 'self-so-ness' of how things work. Understanding this helps you realize your full potential, be less stressed and 'get things right first time.' The related habit is to act authentically in accord with the inevitable dynamics of the cosmos and your surroundings. To build this habit:

   ☐ Avoid overthinking things.
   ☐ Practice and honour your intuition.
   ☐ Don't 'get in your own way.'

4. **Pu** represents simplicity and clarity of understanding. The associated habit is to perceive without prejudice. This reinforces the first three habits. To do this:

   ☐ Consider using meditation to 'fast your heart-mind.'
   ☐ De-program your prejudices.
   ☐ Declutter and simplify your life.

5. **Wuwei** is action without effort or artifice. Acting with *wuwei* helps you cultivate your energies, rather than squander them. To gain these benefits, steps for developing your *wuwei* habit include:

   ☐ Always be naturally and fully 'present' in situations.
   ☐ Nudge yourself into *wuwei* using small experiments.
   ☐ Pause and reflect.

6. **De** is your potency. It is how you radiate your power in a way that fulfils you. It is the North Star to guide you daily in how you co—operate with your dynamic environment. If you are aware of this, you will improve your relationships with others. You will have a more positive effect on them, with the benefits that accrue, both to them and to you. Steps include:

- ☐ Know your values.
- ☐ Know your magic formula, aka your unique ability to add value.
- ☐ Use a sketch or painting to envision and develop your de.

7. **Zhenren** is insightful mastery. By adopting the previous principles, techniques and habits of Daoism, you deliver virtuoso performance and live in flow, fulfilment and resilience.

With practice, we can live these principles in a *ziran* and *wuwei* way – and gain, automatically and spontaneously, the benefits that they bring.

# APPENDIX 1

# HOW DAOISM DEVELOPED

The history of Daoism is like a tree. It has many roots and many branches. It is a bit like the Dao of the cosmos itself: dynamic, evolving, self-organizing, porous, syncretic – bobbing and weaving its way through dramatic eras of China's history.

The core of this book has focused on the trunk of that tree. It has focused on the early yet enduring principles. This Appendix now gives a historical overview of the sources from which Daoism sprang, and the branches that developed after the classical period.

The roots of Daoism lie in the beliefs and practices of ancient China dating back beyond 1,000 BCE. Its core foundations were built from the 6th to the 4th centuries BCE. Across subsequent centuries, Daoism developed the trappings of a religion, although its central philosophies remained intact. It developed as an institution, which sometimes won Imperial support, and at other times lost out to the Confucians or Buddhists.

1. **ANCIENT ROOTS AND *I CHING*** (BEFORE 1,000 BCE–700 BCE)
   Before and during the relative peace of the Western Zhou Dynasty (1,045 BCE–771 BCE), strands of Chinese folk-belief coalesced.

   For this agrarian society, the weather was crucial. A class of shamans emerged who promised to predict rain and drought, and even to compel the former and fend off the latter. These shamans, witch-doctors and soothsayers claimed their powers derived from their communication with the spirit world. This concept was crystallized as Heaven, led by the highest deity, *ShangDi*.

From here sprang early attempts to understand the cosmos. A core idea emerged, which still holds sway in Chinese philosophy, of the importance of harmony and congruence between the three realms of Heaven above, Earth beneath, and Mankind in between. Emperors claimed to rule through the so-called 'Mandate of Heaven,' but in return they had a duty to assure the required harmony between the three realms.

The *Yijing* was written around 1,000 BCE – one of the world's first books. It recorded ideas on divination, cosmology, the central role of *yin-yang*, and the process of pervasive and continuous change. It also applied them to the human predicament. Ideas from the *Yijing* would go on to influence all later thinking on philosophical Daoism. The *Yijing* endured because it provided richer and more subtle answers than earlier divination techniques, and enshrined three points that would have lasting influence.

First was the focus on change. Each hexagram did not represent a static situation; it represented an ecosystem of things that were in flux. This dynamic would become core to Daoist thinking.

Second, this process of flux was emphasized in the metaphysics of the time. This included beliefs about how the cosmos came to be. From Nothing (*wu*) was born the Supreme Ultimate (*tai chi*). From the Supreme Ultimate, *yin* and *yang* emerged spontaneously. The two (*yin* and *yang*), produced the three (Heaven, Earth and Man), and the three produced the 'ten thousand things' – a term that means 'everything.'

Third, as Carl Jung would later observe, the *Yijing* had ceased to be a book of divination, and instead had become a book of *wisdom*. It did not state what the future would be, but rather suggested aspects of the situation that the consulter could consider before choosing a course of action.

In parallel to the workings of the world, the workings of the human body were explored. The body was considered to be a microcosm of the external cosmos, and physicians sought the rules governing how it works. Their findings laid the basis for Traditional Chinese Medicine, and for the processes that we still see today in Daoist meditation techniques, and that are incorporated into the movements of tai chi and qigong.

Powerful currents of belief had thus emerged during this period up to 700 BCE, which would influence Daoism as well as Confucianism and other schools of thought. With the *Yijing* as a grandparent of Daoism, the core tenets of *yin-yang* (the dynamic interplay of complements) and *qi* (vital energy) were set.

## 2. CORE FOUNDATIONS – HUNDRED SCHOOLS OF THOUGHT, LAOZI AND ZHUANGZI (700 BCE-221 BCE)

As the Zhou Dynasty crumbled, discord and anxiety swept China. Regional warlords took control. These leaders of competing states were ready sponsors of wandering scholars and sages who offered strategies promising competitive advantage over neighbouring warlords. Some of these strategies were military – as illustrated by Sun Tzu's *The Art of War*. Other strategies aimed at more effective statecraft, societal codes and personal codes of thought and behaviour.

These factors triggered a period of huge philosophical innovation. Collectively, these wandering sages, including Confucius, created the era that would later be called the Hundred Schools of Thought (ca. 550 BCE-221 BCE). In addition to Daoism, the schools included Confucianism, Mohism and Legalism.

The two most-quoted texts of Daoism appeared during this era, between the 5th and 4th centuries BCE. Supposedly written by the masters Laozi and Zhuangzi, they are almost certainly the work of multiple authors.

The first, *Daodejing* (*Classic of the Way and [Its] Power*), is the most cited book in Daoism. Its 5,000 characters were allegedly written by Laozi. It focuses on two related themes. The first is cosmology, and particularly on the relationship between the Dao and the world. Its second main theme is *wuwei*, advocating an ethic of virtuous, effortless action untethered from desires.

Zhuangzi's eponymous book recounts a string of stories with cutting humour and intellectual curiosity. It addresses the importance of naturalness and sponta-neity (*ziran*), and the nature of existence. The latter topic includes the oft-quoted story in which Zhuangzi awakes from dreaming that he was a butterfly and asks, "Was I Zhuangzi dreaming I was a butterfly, or a butterfly dreaming I was Zhuangzi?"

Other influential texts included *Liezi*, considered the third classic of Daoism, with a strong resemblance to *Zhuangzi*. Recent archaeology and scholarship have ele-vated the importance of other works of similar or earlier age, including *Neiye* (Inward Training – an engaging account of early meditation techniques, and part of the broader *Guanzi*), and *Wenzi*, which contains elements of Confucianism and other schools.

As the Hundred Schools period ended, Confucianism would emerge for several centuries as the dominant soci-etal force in China, though it would also absorb and carry forward elements of Daoist and pre-Daoist thinking.

### 3. FORMALIZATION OF DAOISM (206 BCE–220 CE)

The influential Han Dynasty (206 BCE–220 CE) saw the newly unified China become truly integrated. Daoism was first defined as a discrete tradition by China's Grand Historian, Sima Qian (146–86 BCE). Laozi and Zhuangzi were named as its founders.

Daoism had development in many ways. The hitherto practical-metaphysical Daoism developed a religious and liturgical side, which continues to this day. Laozi was canonized. Religious revelations were announced. Priests and cults accorded themselves grand titles such as The School of Celestial Masters. Alchemy developed from its folk origins to entwine with existing Daoist theories to offer new ways to live a long and healthy life. Classical work from this period included *Huainanzi*, which combined notions of *yin-yang* and *wuxing* with other ideas from the Hundred Schools of Thought, and *Baopuzi* (The Master who Embraces Simplicity).

### 4. EXCHANGES WITH CONFUCIANISM AND BUDDHISM (220–618)

During the next 350 years, both the philosophical and institutional aspects of Daoism continued to develop. The more austere and rigid Confucianism and the more free-wheeling and open Daoism exchanged ideas. But these traditions retained their identities: it was said one should be a Confucian at work and a Daoist at home.

After Buddhism entered China in the first century AD, its transmission accelerated during the 5th and 6th centuries, and well-established Daoist concepts were hijacked to explain and make more familiar the strange imports from India. The venerable and subtle 'Dao' was used as a translation of *dharma* ('teaching'); *wuwei* ('action without artifice') became a translation of Buddhist *nirvana*.

In this way, Daoism as the lingua franca shepherded in Buddhism, but at the same time sowed the seeds for its own later upstaging by it.

Buddhists and Daoists were set for centuries of argument, with Buddhists calling Daoism 'The Way of Demons.' The Daoists retaliated by claiming that Buddhism was anyway founded by their own canonized leader, Laozi, claiming he had gone to India to enlighten the masses in the guise of Buddha. Imperial support seesawed. Sometimes the Daoists were victimized, and at other times it was the Buddhist temples that were burned.

Daoism survived, in part by adopting religious ideas from other faiths. For example, new Daoist schools such as *Lingbao* (Sacred Treasure) and *Shangqing* (Supreme Clarity), now borrowed from folk religion and Confucianism to establish hierarchical theocracies. Daoism also borrowed from Buddhism to include the notion of the afterlife.

The stage was now set for the trend that continues to this day of *san jiao he yi* ('three faiths as one'). Many Chinese people happily practice elements of all three faiths: Daoism, Buddhism and Confucianism.

## 5. GOLDEN AGE, THEN BATTLE FOR POWER (618–1279)

During China's golden age of the Tang Dynasty (618–907), Daoism became the country's official state religion and Laozi's *Daodejing* was at last admitted as one of the classics to be studied for the prestigious civil service examinations. But then, and into the Song Dynasty (960-1279), China's three religions all had to battle for power at court and for funding of temples and monasteries. At this time the 5,000-volume *Daozang* (Daoist canon) was established and copied multiple times.

The Song Dynasty also saw the founding of the *Quanzhen* (Complete Perfection) School. This school mixed Confucian formality, simple asceticism, Buddhist monarchism and Daoist inner alchemy. That mix perhaps explains why it is one of only two surviving formal Daoist Schools (along with The Celestial Masters).

### 6. **SHIFTING FORTUNES** (1279–1912)

When the Mongols conquered China to found the Yuan Dynasty (1279–1367), they brought Tibetan Buddhism with them as the state religion. Daoism was vilified. Almost every copy of its canon was destroyed.

Daoism saw periodic patronage again during the Ming Dynasty (1368–1644) and its canon was recreated in 5,000 volumes. But the tides turned yet again as the Manchus invaded to establish the Qing Dynasty (1644–1912). The Confucians now gained a definitive upper hand, and Daoist texts was again largely destroyed.

The China Nationalists (1912–1949) confiscated and repurposed many of the temples of the Daoist religion that they deemed reactionary. The People's Republic of China (1949–present), during the Cultural Revolution (1966–1976), destroyed many more temples and imprisoned monks and priests. But Daoism has recently become respected again, out of respect for its traditional roots, and many sites have now been restored.

———————

Across this vast sweep of 2,500 years, China's population grew from 40 million to 1,400 million. This brought radical changes to structures of government, the economy and social norms.

These changes affected many aspects of the daily practice of Daoism. There was, for example, greater or lesser emphasis on cosmology, alchemy, meditation, dietary practices, asceticism and liturgy.

Daoism's core principles have, however, endured. These include the seven principles this book focuses on: *yin-yang*, *li*, *pu*, *ziran*, *wuwei*, *de* and *zhenren*.

For further details of Daoism's historical development, see Kirkland's *Taoism: The Enduring Tradition* and his *The History of Taoism: A New Outline*; and Komjathy's *Daoism: A Guide for the Perplexed*, and the introduction in his *Daoist Handbooks*.

# APPENDIX 2

# THE SIX BASIC HUMAN NEEDS

I have found one of the best frameworks for reflecting on one's own human condition to be Tony Robbins' Six Basic Human Needs. It draws from neurolinguistic programming, cognitive therapy, Gestalt Therapy, Maslow's Hierarchy of Needs and more.[90] The focus is on deep psychological needs that drive our emotions, rather than more transient or superficial desires.

Below is a brief summary, including my own pairing of complementary relationships (not opposites), and the notions of Being, Belonging and Becoming.

Reflecting on what these factors mean for you can contribute to refining your *de* potency, and the domain of your *wuwei* (effortless action) and *zhenren* (mastery).

---

90  See, for example, Robbins, A "6 Basic Needs That Make Us Tick." *Entrepreneur Europe.* December 4, (2014). Available at: ttps://www.entrepreneur.com/article/240441

## BEING

**Certainty** – urge to build certainty in your life, to minimize the stress of uncertainty. Need for safety, stability, security, order, predictability, control, consistency

**Uncertainty or Variety** – urge to relieve boredom, predictability and stagnation. Need for novelty, variety, surprise, adventure, challenge, excitement, difference

## BELONGING

**Significance** – urge to gain significance in the eyes of self and others; a sense of identity. Need for meaning, feeling important, worthy, special, proud, needed

**Love and connection** – urge for deep connections with people. Need to love and be loved; to belong. Need for attachment and communication, intimacy

## BECOMING

**Growth** – urge to develop and grow. Need for learning, and for emotional, intellectual and spiritual development

**Contribution** – urge to contribute to something greater than yourself, adding to other people's lives. Need to give to, care for and protect others

# APPENDIX 3

# GLOSSARY AND PRONUNCIATION GUIDE

| PINYIN / MANDARIN | | MEANING | PRONUNCIATION |
|---|---|---|---|
| **7 principles** | | | |
| de | 德 | potency; virtue | halfway between 'ter' and 'der' |
| li | 理 | pattern | 'lee' |
| pu | 樸 | simplicity; clarity | 'poo' |
| wuwei | 無為 | action without artifice; effortless action; action without action | 'woo way' |
| yin-yang | 陰陽 | sunny; projective - shady; receptive | 'yin'-'yaang' |
| zhenren | 真人 | perfected person; a Daoist sage | chenren (ch as in prestige) |
| ziran | 自然 | spontaneous; natural; self-so | churaan (ch as in prestige) |

## Other key terms

| dao | 道 | the way | halfway between 'town' and 'down' without the final 'n' |
|---|---|---|---|
| he | 和 | harmony | 'her' |
| Laozi | 老子 | 'old master'; legendary author of *Daodejing* | 'lao-tzer' |
| long | 龍 | dragon | 'lung' |
| neidan | 內丹 | inner alchemy | 'nay-daan' |
| qi | 氣 | breath, vital energy | 'chee' |
| qigong | 氣功 | form of energy-promoting exercise | 'chigung' |
| xian | 仙 | an immortal (person of the mountains) | 'hshian' |
| xiang sheng | 相生 | mutual arising | 'hshiang sheng' |
| xin | 心 | heart, mind; soul; the seat of personality | 'hshin' |
| Zhuangzi | 莊子 | author and eponymous book | 'chung-zer' (ch as in prestige) |

# ACKNOWLEDGEMENTS

Few books are conceived in a single act, and this is not one of them. Over the decades, many friends, colleagues and clients have contributed many ideas, ranging from intriguing fragments to fundamental insights. To record all that help would require a book in itself. However, I thank and acknowledge the following people in particular.

For their continual offerings of brilliant ideas, I thank: Partha Bose, Ian Davis, Dr Jocelyn Dehnert, Dr Graeme Delort-McNaught, Professor Dominic Houlder, Professor Herminia Ibarra, Ken Landsberg, Olivia Landsberg, Geoff Lloyd, Robert Mack, Dr Elisabeth Marx, Professor Paul O'Prey, Norman Sanson, Dr Anne Scoular, Dr Laura Watkins, and Dr Declan Woods. Thanks in particular to Andrei Stepanov and Dr Jon Stokes, who read early versions of this book.

I also thank my many colleagues from McKinsey, Korn Ferry, and Heidrick & Struggles, who offered valuable input over the years.

For communicating their insights into Chinese religion and philosophy, I gratefully acknowledge the works of Roger Ames, Steven Bokenkamp, Thomas Cleary, Steve Coutinho, David Hall, Chad Hansen, Philip Ivanhoe, Russell Kirkland, Livia Kohn, Louis Komjathy, D.C. Lau, Ronnie Littlejohn, Victor Mair, Fabrizio Pregadio, Isabelle Robinet, Harold Roth, Kristofer Schipper, Edward Slingerland, Eva Wong, Lee Yearley, and Brook Ziporyn, and thank them for permission where I have quoted them.

For sparking the motivation to write down these ideas, and for suggesting major adjustments to the first draft, special thanks go to Roxana Donath and my long-term publishing mentor, Martin Liu.

Thank you also to Martin's editorial team at LID, including Clare Christian, Caroline Li and Teya Ucherdzhieva.

Finally, I acknowledge the seminal contributions of my parents, Peter and Sylvia Landsberg, of happy memory: the older I become, the more I recognize the value of their conversations and role modelling.

# SUGGESTED READING AND BIBLIOGRAPHY

Western scholarship and commentary on Daoism has grown strongly since the 1960s. Reliable scholarly authors include: Roger Ames, Steven Bokenkamp, Thomas Cleary, Steve Coutinho, Mark Csikszentmihalyi, Angus Graham, David Hall, Chad Hansen, Philip Ivanhoe, Russell Kirkland, Livia Kohn, Louis Komjathy, D.C. Lau, Ronnie Littlejohn, Victor Mair, Fabrizio Pregadio, Harold Roth, Isabelle Robinet, Kristofer Schipper, Edward Slingerland, Burton Watson, Alan Watts, Eva Wong, Lee Yearley and Brook Ziporyn.

The sections below offer suggested readings and resources. They cover: introductions to Daoism; the Daoist Classics; Daoism lived in broader contexts; Flow; Chengyu and other pithy Chinese expressions; Tools for when you can't speak Chinese; and Journals on Daoism. These exclude modern commentaries written in Chinese.

## INTRODUCTIONS TO DAOISM

*The Watercourse Way* by Alan Watts remains a favourite introduction to the essence of Daoism, from its foremost expositor to the West. Unencumbered by historical and religious explanations, it gets to the heart of the principles of Daoism. Watts' lectures can be found online in many podcasts and videos.

*Daodejing* by Chih-Chung Tsai brings Daoism to life by illustrating the classic *Daodejing* in cartoon format.

*The Encyclopedia of Taoism*, edited by Fabrizio Pregadio, contains 800 entries by respected experts, covering Daoist religion, thought and history.

*Dao Companion to Chinese Philosophy*, edited by Xiaogan Liu, is a comprehensive introduction to Daoist Philosophy, including analyses by top scholars in the field. It is Volume 6 of Springer's 16-volume series examining various aspects of Chinese Philosophy.

Online, **Stanford University's Plato site** offers good overviews, being part of Stanford's Encyclopedia of Philosophy, which 'organizes scholars from around the world in philosophy and related disciplines to create and maintain an up-to-date reference work.' https://plato.stanford.edu/entries/daoism/

The **Internet Encyclopedia of Philosophy** contains helpful entries on Daoism, and on specific aspects of it (such as *wuwei*) – as well as on related aspects of Chinese thinking such as Confucianism. https://iep.utm.edu/daoismdaoist-philosophy/

*Introducing Daoism* by Livia Kohn, who has written or edited more than 35 books on the subject, is a broad introduction – going beyond philosophy to include the historical, religious and longevity-seeking aspects of Daoism.

At the time of writing, the following site outlines the development of Western commentary on Daoism: http://esoteric.msu.edu/VolumeVI/Dao.htm

## THE DAOIST CLASSICS

*Daodejing* attributed to Laozi. The first holistic classic of Daoism, from the 4th century BCE, starts with the famously enigmatic line, "The Dao that can be spoken of is not the eternal Dao." Nevertheless, the book sets out the essence of Daoism over 81 related verses.

As the most-translated book after the Bible, first translated into English in 1868, and now in more than 250 Western languages, it exists in many print and freely available online versions. Versions range in terms of scholarly reliability, poeticness and authorial style, including:

- *Dao De Jing* by Tsai Chih-chung, Brian Bruya and Pico Iyer [excellent cartoon format].
- *Dao De Jing: the Definitive Edition* by Jonathan Star [includes character-by-character translation].
- *Dao De Jing* by D.C. Lau [reliable and scholarly translation].
- *Getting Right with Tao* by Ron Hogan (wonderful rendition in colloquial-speak).
- *The Tao of Power: Lao Tzu's Classic Guide to Leadership, Influence, and Excellence* by R. L. Wing (addresses the book's application to management, leadership and relationships).
- *The Tao Te Ching* by James Legge [one of the earliest translations].
- **Online versions** include a good public domain translation generously donated in 1996 by J.H. McDonald (Googleable).
- **A side-by-side translation** from James Legge, including the original Chinese text and a translation of each character by hovering exists at https://www.yellowbridge.com/onlinelit/daodejing.php and https://ctext.org/dao-de-jing.

- **5 versions side-by-side** are here: https://ttc.tasuki.org/display:Code:gff,sm,jhmd,rh/section:meta.
- **24 versions compared line by line** are here: https://web.archive.org/web/20070630005206/http://www.wayist.org/ttc%20compared/chap01.htm#top.

*Zhuangzi*, attributed to Zhuangzi, is roughly contemporary with *Daodejing* but very different in flavour. It presents the way of the Dao through witty and cutting stories, including the Butterfly story already mentioned in the chapter on *pu* simplicity in this book.

- ***Zhuangzi: The Complete Writings*** by Brook Ziporyn. (Scholarly and accurate; the 2020 edition translates all the chapters; the 2009 edition excludes some.)
- ***Chuang-tzu: The Inner Chapters and Other Writings from the Book of Chuang-tzu***, by A.C. Graham. (Scholarly, with excellent supporting material, but excludes some chapters, and reorganizes others in an unfamiliar way.)
- ***Wandering on the Way: Early Taoist Tales and Parables of Chuang Tzu*** by Victor H. Mair. (The gold standard for years, though now feels a bit dated.)
- ***Wandering at Ease in the Zhuangzi***, edited by scholar Roger T. Ames. (Presents penetrating essays on specific aspects of the *Zhuangzi*, and stories from it.)
- **A side-by-side translation** from James Legge, including the original Chinese text and a translation of each character by hovering exists at https://ctext.org/zhuangzi

*Yijing* aka *Yi* Jing and *I Ching* was written by multiple authors dating back before 1,000 BCE. It originated as a book of divination, but developed into a book of wisdom that offers potential pointers to action in challenging stations. It became more influential after the addition of its 'wings' (appendices) after the 3rd to 6th centuries BCE.

There are many online and print translations of the *Yijing*. As with translations of other Chinese classics, there is wide variation in the degree of scholarship employed, the literalness of the translation, and the quality of the author's commentary. Specifically for the *Yijing*, there are also considerable differences in whether the translation is directive (telling the reader what to do) versus reflection-inducing (flagging up considerations for the reader to notice and reflect upon).

Most interested readers possess several different versions, of which the following are respected by most:

- ***The I Ching or Book of Changes*** by Richard Wilhelm, Cary F. Baynes, Hellmut Wilhelm, C. G. Jung. (Forward by Carl Jung, and introduction by eminent scholar Hellmut Wilhelm, who discusses his father's foundational translation, and recent studies of the I Ching.)
- ***I Ching Workbook*** by R.L. Wing. (Concise format that fosters the reader's exploration, yet reasonably comprehensive as a first introduction.)
- ***The Living I Ching: Using Ancient Chinese Wisdom to Shape Your Life*** by Ming-Dao Deng. (Open-ended and imaginative, conveying the rich symbolism effectively.)
- ***The I Ching or Book of Changes: A Guide to Life's Turning Points*** by Brian Browne Walker. (Clear language, albeit some find it too directive.)
- For a side-by-side translation, including Chinese original text and James Legge's 1899 translation, and the meaning of each character by hovering, see https://www.yellowbridge.com/onlinelit/yijing.php.

## OTHER CLASSICS OF DAOISM INCLUDE:

- *Liezi* [The third, more practical classic of Daoism; roughly contemporary with *Daodejing* and *Zhuangzi*); *Huainanzi* (2nd century BCE, blending Confucian and Legalist concepts with Daoist ones).]
- Ctext.org presents all the classics, though only some are translated into English: https://ctext.org/pre-qin-and-han
- *Neiye* ['Inward Training', 4th century BCE, on personal cultivation through breath control, meditation and *qi* circulation.]

## DAOISM LIVED IN BROADER CONTEXTS

Daoism lives through many practices, as illustrated by the following texts illustrating its relationship to painting, other arts, kung fu and qigong:
- *The Way of Chinese Painting* by Mai-mai Sze
- *Taoism and the Arts of China* by Stephen Little
- *Be Water, My Friend: The True Teachings of Bruce Lee*, by Bruce's sister, Shannon Lee
- *Vital Breath of the Dao: Chinese Shamanic Tiger Qigong* by Zhongxian Wu

## FLOW

Daoism's *wuwei* is intimately related to the flow state. Contemporary classics on flow include:
- *Beyond Boredom and Anxiety: Experiencing Flow in Work and Play* and *Flow: The Psychology of Optimal Experience* by Mihaly Csikszentmihalyi
- *Trying Not to Try* by Edward Slingerland
- *Thinking, Fast and Slow* by Nobel Prize winner Daniel Kahneman

## CHENGYU AND OTHER PITHY CHINESE EXPRESSIONS

You will recall from the titles of this book's chapters that the Chinese language has a knack for compressing a whole world of ideas into a single four-character expression (called *chengyu*). Googling *chengyu* will take you to many sites that offer lengthy lists of them. Examples include:

- https://www.chinasage.info/proverbs/proverbs.htm
- https://chengyu.qianp.com/ (Right-click > Translate to English.)

## TOOLS FOR WHEN YOU CAN'T SPEAK CHINESE!

You can enjoy exploring Chinese characters and texts without being a speaker of Mandarin. Useful resources are:

- **Yellowbridge** is a very useful online English-Chinese dictionary. It also offers a simplified etymology of Chinese characters
  https://www.yellowbridge.com/chinese/dictionary.php.
- **MDBG** also offers a good interface https://www.mdbg.net/chinese/dictionary
- **A fascinating 3,000-year timeline** of how each Chinese character developed from the Shang Dynasty (1,250–1,046 BCE) onwards is available by pasting the character into the following site: https://hanziyuan.net/

## JOURNALS ON DAOISM

Respected academic journals include the following:

- *Daoism* is "a peer-reviewed international journal offering original research articles that explore Daoism in its social and historical contexts from the pre-modern to the contemporary period".
https://cup.cuhk.edu.hk/index.php?route=product/product&product_id=3077

- The *Journal of Chinese Philosophy* is "devoted to the scholarly and creative study of Chinese philosophy and thought, in all phases and stages of articulation and development."
https://onlinelibrary.wiley.com/journal/15406253

- The *Journal of Chinese Religions* is "the longest-standing journal in the field of Chinese religions. It is a peer-reviewed, biannual academic journal that publishes research articles, book reviews and other communications on all aspects of Chinese religions."
https://www.press.jhu.edu/journals/journal-chinese-religions

- The *Journal of Daoist Studies* is an annual publication "dedicated to the scholarly exploration of Daoism in all its different dimensions: history, philosophy, art, society, and more; includes publications, dissertations, conferences and websites."
https://uhpress.hawaii.edu/category/journals/journal-of-daoist-studies/

- *Philosophy East and West* "promotes academic literacy on non-Western traditions of philosophy. Highest-quality scholarship that locates these cultures in their relationship to Anglo-American philosophy."
https://uhpress.hawaii.edu/title/pew/

# BIBLIOGRAPHY

Note that some texts use alternative spellings – e.g., for *Daodejing* (*Tao Te Ching*; *Dao De Jing*); *Zhuangzi* (*Chuang Tzu*), *Liezi* (*Lieh Tzu*) and *Yijing* (*I Ching*).

Allen, David. *Getting Things Done: The Art of Stress-Free Productivity*. London: Piatkus, 2019.

Arthur, Brian W. "Decisions, Decisions." *FastCompany Magazine*. 30 September 1998. Retrieved 26 September 2022 from https://www.fastcompany.com/35023/decisions-decisions.

Baron, Robert A. "Opportunity Recognition as Pattern Recognition: How Entrepreneurs 'Connect the Dots' to Identify New Business Opportunities." *Academy of Management Perspectives* 20, no. 1 (February 2006): 104–19. https://doi.org/10.5465/amp.2006.19873412.

Baron, Robert A. "Opportunity Recognition: A Cognitive Perspective." *Academy of Management Proceedings* 2004, no. 1 (August 2004): A1–6. https://doi.org/10.5465/ambpp.2004.13862818.

Basso, Julia C., Alexandra McHale, Victoria Ende, Douglas J. Oberlin, and Wendy A. Suzuki. "Brief, Daily Meditation Enhances Attention, Memory, Mood, and Emotional Regulation in Non-Experienced Meditators." *Behavioural Brain Research* 356 (January 2019): 208–20. https://doi.org/10.1016/j.bbr.2018.08.023.

Borges, Jorge Luis. *Collected Fictions*. Translated by Andrew Hurley. New York: Penguin Books, 1999. Chapter: "The Library of Babel."

Brown, Joshua, and Alexus McLeod. *Transcendence and Non-Naturalism in Early Chinese Thought*. London: Bloomsbury Publishing Plc, Bloomsbury Academic, 2021.

Burton, Damon, and Cheryl Weiss. "The Fundamental Goal Concept: The Path to Process and Performance Success." In T. S. Horn (Ed.), *Advances in Sport Psychology*, Human Kinetics, 2008. (pp. 339–375, 470–474).

Campbell, Cary. "Educating Openness: Umberto Eco's Poetics of Openness as a Pedagogical Value." *Signs and Society* 6, no. 2 (March 2018): 305–31. https://doi.org/10.1086/695567.

Campbell, Joseph. *The Hero with a Thousand Faces*. Novalto: New World Library, 2008.

Chapman, Elizabeth N., Anna Kaatz, and Molly Carnes. "Physicians and Implicit Bias: How Doctors May Unwittingly Perpetuate Health Care Disparities." *Journal of General Internal Medicine* 28, no. 11 (11 April, 2013): 1504–10. https://doi.org/10.1007/s11606-013-2441-1.

Charness, Neil, Anders Ericsson, Robert R. Hoffman, Aaron Kozbelt, and A. Mark Williams, eds. *The Cambridge Handbook of Expertise and Expert Performance*. Cambridge: Cambridge University Press, 2018.

Chatwin, Jonathan. 2016. "The Enduring Influence of the I Ching." http://www. thatsmags.com/beijing/post/12010/i-ching. Accessed 26 September 2022.

Christian, Brian, and Tom Griffiths. *Algorithms to Live by: The Computer Science of Human Decisions*. New York: Picador: Henry Holt and Company, 2017.

CIPD Factsheet 2009. "Mentoring." Available at: https://www.cipd.co.uk/knowledge/ fundamentals/people/development/coaching-mentoring-factsheet

Cline, E. M. "Mirrors, Minds, and Metaphors." *Philosophy East and West* 58, no. 3 (2008): 337–357. https://doi.org/10.1353/pew.0.0006.

Cline, Erin M. "How to Fish Like a Daoist." In *Riding the Wind with Liezi: New Essays on the Daoist Classic*, edited by Ronnie Littlejohn and Jeffrey Dippmann, 225–40. Albany: State University of New York Press, 2011.

Clutterbuck, David. *Everyone Needs a Mentor*. London: Chartered Institute of Personnel and Development, 2014.

Collins, James C. *Good to Great: Why Some Companies Make the Leap and Others Don't*. London: Random House Business Books, 2013. https://doi. org/10.1177/0974173920090719.

Collins, James C. *Built to Last: Successful Habits of Visionary Companies*. Paw Prints, 2011.

Cooper, Jean Campbell. *An Illustrated Encyclopaedia of Traditional Symbols*. London: Thames and Hudson, 1978.

Coutinho, Steve. *An Introduction to Daoist Philosophies*. New York: Columbia University Press, 2014.

Covey, Stephen R. *The 7 Habits of Highly Effective People*. London: Simon & Schuster UK Ltd, 2020.

Csikszentmihalyi, Mihaly. *Flow: The Psychology of Optimal Experience*. New York: Harper and Row, 1990.

Davis, Bryan. "The Power of Knowledge-Pattern Recognition." Chapter 4 in Nick Bontis (editor) *World Congress on Intellectual Capital Readings*. Boston: Butterworth-Heinemann, 2002.

De Bono, Edward. *Six Thinking Hats*. London: Penguin Life, an imprint of Penguin Books, 2017.

Dewar, Carolyn. "Culture: 4 keys to why it matters." Retrieved 24 November 2022 from www.mckinsey.com/capabilities/people-and-organizational-performance/ our-insights/the-organization-blog/culture-4-keys-to-why-it-matters.

Dunning, David. *Self-Insight: Roadblocks and Detours on the Path to Knowing Thyself*. New York: Psychology Press, 2005.

Ellis, Albert. *How to Make Yourself Happy and Remarkably Less Disturbable*. Atascadero, Calif: Impact Publishers, 2007.

Eno, Robert. *Zhuangzi: The Inner Chapters*, 2019. URI: https://hdl.handle. net/2022/23427, Open access at: https://terebess.hu/english/Zhuangzi-Eno.pdf.

Erikson, Erik H. *Psychological Issues*. New York, NY: International University Press, 1959.

Feynman, Richard P., and Anthony Zee. *QED: The Strange Theory of Light and Matter*. Princeton, NJ: Princeton University Press, 2014.

Feynman, Richard P., and Edward Hutchings. *"Surely You're Joking, Mr. Feynman!"*: *Adventures of Curious Character*. New York: W. W. Norton, 1997.

Fuller, Michael Anthony. *An Introduction to Chinese Poetry: From the Canon of Poetry to the Lyrics of the Song Dynasty*. Cambridge, Massachusetts: Published by Harvard University Asia Center, 2018.

Gerritsen, Roderik. J. S., and Guido P. H. Band. "Breath of Life: The Respiratory Vagal Stimulation Model of Contemplative Activity." *Frontiers in Human Neuroscience* 12 (9 October, 2018). https://doi.org/10.3389/fnhum.2018.00397.

Gigerenzer, Gerd, and Peter M. Todd. *Simple Heuristics That Make Us Smart*. New York: Oxford University Press, 2001.

Goldsmith, Marshall. *What Got You Here Won't Get You There: How Successful People Become Even More Successful*. London: Profile, 2011.

Goldsmith, Marshall and Mark Reiter. *The Earned Life: Lose Regret, Choose Fulfillment*. New York: Currency, 2022.

Goleman, Daniel. *Emotional Intelligence*. Bloomsbury Publishing, 2020.

Gombrich, Ernst Hans. *Art and Illusion*. London: Phaidon, 1977.

Gould, Daniel, Robert C. Eklund, and Susan A. Jackson. "Coping Strategies Used by U.S. Olympic Wrestlers." *Research Quarterly for Exercise and Sport*. 64, no. 1 (March, 1993): 83–93. https://doi.org/10.1080/02701367.1993.10608782.

Graham, Angus Charles. *Book of Lieh-Tzu*. New York: Columbia University Press, 1990.

Graham, Angus Charles. *Chuang-Tzu: The Inner Chapters and Other Writings from the Book of Chuang-Tzu*. London: Unwin Paperbacks, 1986.

Groysberg, Boris, Jeremiah Lee, Jesse Price, and J. Cheng. "The Leader's Guide to Corporate Culture." *Harvard Business Review* 96, no. 1 (2018): 44–52.

Han, Ying. *Han Shi Wai Zhuan: The Outer Commentary to the Book of Songs by Master Han*. See https://ctext.org/han-shi-wai-zhuan/juan-qi.

Haselton, Martie G., Daniel Nettle, and Paul W. Andrews. "The Evolution of Cognitive Bias." 724–746. Chapter in Buss, David M. *The Handbook of Evolutionary Psychology*. Hoboken, New Jersey: John Wiley & Sons, Inc., 2015.

Hodges, Nicola J., and A. M. Williams. *Skill Acquisition in Sport: Research, Theory and Practice*. London; New York: Routledge, an imprint of the Taylor & Francis Group, 2020.

Hoff, Benjamin, and Ernest H. Shepard. *The Tao of Pooh and, the Te of Piglet*. London: Egmont UK Limited, 2019.

Hogan, Ron. *Getting Right with Tao: A Contemporary Spin on the Tao Te Ching*. New York: Channel V Books, 2010.

Hon, Tze-ki. "Coping with Contingency and Uncertainty: The Yijing Hexagrams on Decay and Discordance." *Sungkyun Journal of East Asian Studies* 19, no. 1 (2019): 1–17. https://doi.org/10.21866/esjeas.2019.19.1.001.

Hua, Sam. *Sun Tzu's Art of War: A Modern Exposition*. Lid Editorial Empresarial S.L., 2021. Chapter 10.

Ivanhoe, Philip J. "Early Confucianism and Environmental Ethics." In *Confucianism and Ecology: The Interrelation of Heaven, Earth, and Humans*, edited by Mary Evelyn Tucker and John Berthrong, 59–76. Cambridge, Mass.: Harvard University Press, 1998.

Ivanhoe, Philip J. "Human Beings and Nature in Traditional Chinese Thought." In *A Companion to World Philosophies*, edited by Eliot Deutsch and Ronald Bontekoe, 155–64. Oxford: Blackwell, 1997.

Ivanhoe, Philip J. "The Concept of De ('Virtue') in the Laozi." *In Religious and Philosophical Aspects of the Laozi*, edited by Mark Csikszentmihalyi and Philip J. Ivanhoe, 239–57. Albany: State University of New York Press, 1999.

Ivanhoe, Philip J. "The Theme of Unselfconsciousness in the Liezi." In *Riding the Wind with Liezi: New Essays on the Daoist Classic*, edited by Ronnie Littlejohn and Jeffrey Dippmann, 129–52. Albany: State University of New York Press, 2011.

Ivanhoe, Philip J. "The Values of Spontaneity." In *Taking Confucian Ethics Seriously: Contemporary Theories and Applications*, edited by Yu Kam-por, Julia Tao, and Philip J. Ivanhoe, 183–207. Albany: State University of New York Press, 2010.

Ivanhoe, Philip J. *The Daodejing of Laozi*. Indianapolis: Hackett Publishing Company, 2002.

Ivanhoe, Philip J., and Bryan William Van Norden. *Readings in Classical Chinese Philosophy*. Indianapolis: Hackett Publishing, 2007.

James Legge. *The Sacred Books of China: The Texts of Taoism, Translated by James Legge*. Oxford, Clarendon Press, 1891. Series: Sacred Books of the East, v. 39–40.

Jung, Carl. G. *Memories, Dreams, Reflections*. London: William Collins, 2019.

Kahneman, Daniel *Thinking, Fast and Slow*. London: Penguin, 2011.

Kipling Rudyard. *Rudyard Kipling's Verse, Inclusive ed.* Whitefish Mont: Kessinger Publishing, 2012.

Kirkland, R. "The History of Taoism: A New Outline." *Journal of Chinese Religions* 30, no. 1 (September 2002): 177–193. https://doi.org/10.1179/073776902804760257.

Kirkland. *Taoism: The Enduring Tradition*. London and New York: Routledge, 2004.

Kohn, Livia. Entry *wuwei*. In Fabrizio Pregadio ed. *Encyclopedia of Taoism*. London: Routledge, 2008.

Kohn, Livia. *Introducing Daoism*. London: Routledge, 2009.

Kohn, Livia. *Zhuangzi: Text and Context*. St. Petersburg (Fla.): Three Pines Press, 2014.

Komjathy, Louis. *Daoism: A Guide for the Perplexed*. London: Bloomsbury, 2014.

Komjathy, Louis. *Handbooks for Daoist Practice*. Hong Kong: Yuen Yuen Institute, 2008.

Lai, Karen L. "Understanding Change: The Interdependent Self in Its Environment." *Journal of Chinese Philosophy* 34, no. 5 (19 February, 2007): 81–99. https://doi.org/10.1163/15406253-03405007.

Lai, Karyn L., and Wai Wai Chiu. *Skill and Mastery: Philosophical Stories from the Zhuangzi*. London: Rowman & Littlefield International, 2019. Chapter 2.

Landsberg, Max. *Mastering Coaching: Practical Insights for Developing High Performance*. London: Profile Books, 2015.

Landsberg, Max. *The Call of the Mountains: Sights and Inspirations from a Journey of a Thousand Miles Across Scotland's Munros*. Edinburgh: Luath Press, 2018.

Landsberg, Max. *The Tao of Coaching*. London: Profile Books, 2015.

Landsberg, Max. *The Tools of Leadership: Vision, Inspiration, Momentum*. London: Profile Books, 2003.

Lau, Dim-cheuk. *Tao Te Ching*. Hong Kong: Chinese Univ. Press, 1982.

Lauritzen, D. V., F. S. Hertel, L. K. Jordan, and M. S. Gordon. "Salmon Jumping: Behavior, Kinematics and Optimal Conditions, with Possible Implications for Fish Passageway Design." *Bioinspiration & Biomimetics* 5, no. 3 (20 August, 2010): 035006. https://doi.org/10.1088/1748-3182/5/3/035006.

Lavretsky, H., E. S. Epel, P. Siddarth, N. Nazarian, N. St. Cyr, D. S. Khalsa, J. Lin, E. Blackburn, and M. R. Irwin. "A Pilot Study of Yogic Meditation for Family Dementia Caregivers with Depressive Symptoms: Effects on Mental Health, Cognition, and Telomerase Activity." *International Journal of Geriatric Psychiatry* 28, no. 1 (11 March, 2012): 57–65. https://doi.org/10.1002/gps.3790.

Lee, Shannon. *Be Water, My Friend: The True Teachings of Bruce Lee*. London: Rider, 2020.

Legge, James. *Tao Te Ching*. Simon & Brown, 2018.

Levin, Daniel Z., Jorge Walter, and J. Keith Murnighan. "The Power of Reconnection: How Dormant Ties Can Surprise You." *MIT Sloan Management Review* 52, no. 3 (2011): 45.

Little, Stephen, and Shawn Eichman. *Taoism and the Arts of China*. Chicago: Art Institute of Chicago, 2000.

Liu, Xiaogan ed. *Dao Companion to Daoist Philosophy*. 6. Dordrecht: Springer Nederlands, 2014. https://doi.org/10.1007/978-90-481-2927-0.

Maguire, Eleanor A., David G. Gadian, Ingrid S. Johnsrude, Catriona D. Good, John Ashburner, Richard SJ Frackowiak, and Christopher D. Frith. "Navigation-related Structural Change in the Hippocampi of Taxi Drivers." *Proceedings of the National Academy of Sciences* 97, no. 8 (2000): 4398-4403.

Mair, Victor H. *Wandering on the Way: Early Taoist Tales and Parables of Chuang Tzu*. Honolulu: Univ. of Hawai'i Press, 2006.

Major, John S. *The Essential Huainanzi*. New York: Columbia University Press, 2012.

Marlowe, Christopher. *Doctor Faustus*. Act V Sc 2 In Jump, John D. *Marlowe: Doctor Faustus*. London: Macmillan, 1969.

Maslow Abraham H. *Motivation and Personality*. Harper & Row, 1974.

Mason, Elinor, and Rosalind Hursthouse. "On Virtue Ethics." *Utilitas*. 2003 Jul 1;15(02):250-251. https://doi.org/10.1017/S095382080000399X.

Matko, Karin, and Peter Sedlmeier. "What is Meditation? PROPOSING an Empirically Derived Classification System." *Frontiers in Psychology* 10 (2019): 2276. DOI 10.3389/fpsyg.2019.02276.

Mattson, Mark P. "Superior Pattern Processing is the Essence of the Evolved Human Brain." *Frontiers in Neuroscience* (2014): 265.

McDonald, J.H. *"Tao Te Ching Written by Lao-Tzu."* 1996. A translation for the public domain. https://terebess.hu/english/tao/mcdonald.html.

McDonald, Kirk T. 2013. "Can Salmon Swim up a Waterfall after Leaping into It?" Joseph Henry Laboratories, Princeton University, Princeton, NJ Accessed at: http://kirkmcd.princeton.edu/examples/salmon.pdf. Accessed 27 December 2022.

McKee, Robert. *Story: Substance, Structure, Style, and the Principles of Screenwriting.* London: Methuen, 2014.

Mengzi (=Mencius). *Gong Sun Chou 2.* Accessed at: https://ctext.org/mengzi/gong-sun-chou-ii (trans. James Legge).

Ming-Dao, Deng. *The Living I Ching: Using Ancient Chinese Wisdom to Shape Your Life.* San Francisco: Harper San Francisco, 2006.

Miura, Kunio. Entry: *zhenren.* In Fabrizio Pregadio ed. *Encyclopedia of Taoism.* London: Routledge, 2008.

Newton, Isaac, Florian. Cajori, and Andrew. Motte. *Sir Isaac Newton's Mathematical Principles of Natural Philosophy and His System of the World,* 2022.

Osborne, M. F. M. "The Hydrodynamical Performance of Migratory Salmon." *Journal of Experimental Biology* 38, no. 2 (1 June, 1961): 365–90. https://doi.org/10.1242/jeb.38.2.365.

Peng, Kaiping, Julie Spencer-Rodgers, and Zhong Nian. "Naïve Dialecticism and the Tao of Chinese Thought." In Kim, U., Yang, K., Hwang, K. (eds.). *Indigenous and Cultural Psychology,* pp. 247–262. Springer, Boston, MA, 2006.

Pregadio, Fabrizio ed. *Encyclopedia of Taoism.* London: Routledge, 2008.

Purkiss, John. *The Power of Letting Go: How to Drop Everything That's Holding You Back.* London: Aster, an imprint of Octopus Publishing Group, 2020.

Robbins, Anthony, *Awaken the Giant Within: Take Immediate Control of Your Mental, Emotional, Physical and Financial Destiny.* London: Simon & Schuster, Limited, 2012.

Robbins, Tony. "6 Basic Needs That Make Us Tick." *Entrepreneur Europe.* 4 December, 2014. Available at: https://www.entrepreneur.com/article/240441.

Robinson, Andrew. "Did Einstein Really Say That?" *Nature.* 30 April 2018. Retrieved from: https://www.nature.com/articles/d41586-018-05004-4.

Roger T. Ames ed. *Wandering at Ease in the Zhuangzi.* Albany: State University of New York Press, 1998.

Roth, Harold D. "Evidence for Stages of Meditation in Early Taoism." *Bulletin of the School of Oriental and African Studies* 60, no. 2 (June 1997): 295–314. https://doi.org/10.1017/s0041977x00036405.

Roth, Harold D. "The Laozi in the Context of Early Daoist Mystical Praxis." In *Religious and Philosophical Aspects of the Laozi,* edited by Mark Csikszentmihalyi and Philip J. Ivanhoe, 59-96. Albany: State University of New York Press, 1999. 59  96.

Roth, Harold D. "The Yellow Emperor's Guru: A Narrative Analysis from Chuang Tzu 11." *Taoist Resources* 7, no. 1 (1997): 43.

Roth, Harold D. *Original Tao: Inward Training (Nei-yeh) and the Foundations of Taoist Mysticism.* New York: Columbia University Press, 1999.

Sameroff, Arnold. "A Unified Theory of Development: A Dialectic Integration of Nature and Nurture." *Child Development* 81, no. 1 (2010): 6–22.

Saposnik, Gustavo, Donald Redelmeier, Christian C. Ruff, and Philippe N. Tobler. "Cognitive Biases Associated with Medical Decisions: A Systematic Review." *BMC Medical Informatics and Decision Making* 16, no. 1 (2016): 1–14. https://doi.org/10.1186/s12911-016-0377-1.

Seneca, *De Brevitate Vitae.* [Author's translations].

Sekida, Kazuki, and A. V. Grimstone, ed. *Zen Training: Methods and Philosophy.* Boston: Shambhala, 2005.

Shellenbarger, Sue, "Multitasking Makes You Stupid: Studies Show Pitfalls of Doing Too Much at Once," *Wall Street Journal* (27 February, 2003), D1.

Shelley, Percy Bysshe. *The Complete Poetical Works of Percy Bysshe Shelley.* Vol. 2, edited by Thomas Hutchinson. Oxford University Press, 1914. pp. 546–49.

Sinclair, Marta, ed. *Handbook of Research Methods on Intuition.* Cheltenham, UK: Edward Elgar Publishing Limited, 2014.

Slingerland, Edward. "Effortless Action: The Chinese Spiritual Ideal of Wu-wei." *Journal of the American Academy of Religion.* 68 (2000–2): 293–327.

Slingerland, Edward. *Trying Not to Try.* Edinburgh: Canongate, 2015.

Slywotzky, Adrian J., David J. Morrison, Ted Moser, Kevin A. Mundt, and James A. Quella. *Profit Patterns: 30 Ways to Anticipate and Profit from Strategic Forces Reshaping Your Business.* New York: Times Business, 1999.

Speca, Michael, Linda E. Carlson, Eileen Goodey, and Maureen Angen. "A Randomized, Wait-List Controlled Clinical Trial: The Effect of a Mindfulness Meditation-Based Stress Reduction Program on Mood and Symptoms of Stress in Cancer Outpatients." *Psychosomatic Medicine* 62, no. 5 (September 2000): 613–622. https://doi.org/10.1097/00006842-200009000-00004.

Star, Jonathan. *Dao De Jing: The Definitive Edition.* New York: Jeremy P. Tarcher/ Putnam, 2001.

Sun, Bin, Roger T. Ames, and D. C. Lau. *Sun Pin: The Art of Warfare.* New York: Ballantine Books, 1996.

Sun, Tzu. *The Art of War.* Accessed at https://ctext.org/art-of-war/terrain (trans. Lionel Giles).

Sun, Yiping. "On the Characteristics and Modern Relevance of the Taoist Concept of Happiness." *Journal of Zhejiang University (Humanities and Social Sciences Edition)* Vol. 41, No. 1 (2011).

Sze, Mai-mai. *The Way of Chinese Painting.* New York: Vintage Books, 1959.

Tang, Yi-Yuan, Yan Tang, Rongxiang Tang, and Jarrod A. Lewis-Peacock. "Brief Mental Training Reorganizes Large-Scale Brain Networks." *Frontiers in Systems Neuroscience* 11 (28 February, 2017). https://doi.org/10.3389/fnsys.2017.00006.

Tang, Yi-Yuan, Yinghua Ma, Junhong Wang, Yaxin Fan, Shigang Feng, Qilin Lu, Qingbao Yu et al. "Short-term Meditation Training Improves Attention and

Self-regulation." *Proceedings of the National Academy of Sciences* 104, no. 43 (2007): 17152–17156.

Thompson, Kirill O. "'Fallingwater': Daoist Inklings About Place, Strategy, Design, and Space." *International Communication of Chinese Culture* 4, no. 1 (2017): 5–23.

Tsai, Chih-chung, Brian Bruya and Pico Iyer. *Dao De Jing*. Princeton, New Jersey: Princeton University Press, 2020.

US Bureau of Labour Statistics. "American Time Use Survey – May to December 2019 And 2020 Results." USDL–21–1359. Released July 22, 2021. https://www.bls.gov/news.release/pdf/atus.pdf

Walker, Brian B. *The I Ching or Book of Changes: A Guide to Life's Turning Points*. New York: St. Martin's Griffin, 1992.

Watson, Burton. *The Complete Works of Chuang Tzu*. New York: Columbia University Press, 2002.

Watts, Alan W. *The Way of Zen*. New York: Vintage Books, 1957.

Watts, Alan W. and Al Chung-liang Huang. Tao: *The Watercourse Way*. London: Souvenir Press, 2011.

Watts, Alan W. *Psychotherapy East & West*. New York: Ballantine Books, 1974.

Webb, Caroline. *How to Have a Good Day*. London: Pan Books, 2017.

Wen, Kang. *Heroic Tales of Sons and Daughters - 儿女英雄传. - Ernü Yingxiong Zhuan*. Flourished 1821-1850. Chapter 34.

Werner E. T. C. *Myths & Legends of China*. London: Sinclair Browne, 1984.

Wieger, Léon. *Chinese Characters: Their Origin, Etymology, History, Classification and Signification, a Thorough Study from Chinese Documents*. New York: Paragon Book, 1965.

Wilhelm Richard and Cary F Baynes. *The I Ching: or Book of Changes*. 3rd ed. Princeton N.J: Princeton University Press, 1997.

Wilhelm, Richard, Cary F. Baynes, Carl Gustav Jung, and Hellmut Wilhelm. *The I Ching or Book of Changes*. Princeton: Princeton University Press, 1990.

Wing, R. L. *The I Ching Workbook*. New York, NY: Broadway Books, 2001.

Wing, R. L. *The Tao of Power: A Translation of the Tao Te Ching by Lao Tzu*. Garden City, N.Y.: Doubleday, 1986.

Wu, Yuan-tai. (flourished 1522–1526). *Journey to the East*. Public domain: https://gj.zdic.net/archive.php?aid-26912.html.

Wu, Zhongxian. *Vital Breath of the Dao: Chinese Shamanic Tiger Qigong - Laohu Gong*. Singing Dragon, 2012.

Xie He 謝赫, *Gu Huapin Lu* 古畫品錄, *Siku Quanshu* vol. 812, 1b.

Xing, Tao, and Jianghong Ji, *Historical Stories of Chinese Idioms: Zhonghua cheng yu gu shi quan ji*. Beijing: Beijing chu ban she, 2005. Originally by Guo Ruoxu (b 960, d.1127). [Author's translation and adaptation].

Yagoda, Ben. 2018. "Your Lying Mind." *The Atlantic Magazine*. September 2018.

Yearley, Lee H. "The Perfected Person in the Radical Zhuangzi." In Victor H. Mair ed. *Experimental Essays on Zhuangzi*. Dunedin, Fla.: Three Pines Press, 2010. pp 122–36.

Yearley. Lee H. 1996. "Zhuangzi's Understanding of Skillfulness and the Ultimate Spiritual State," in Kjellberg, Paul, and Philip J. Ivanhoe. eds. *Essays on Skepticism, Relativism and Ethics in the Zhuangzi*. New York: State University of New York Press, 1996. Pp. 152–182.

Yeats, W. B., David R. Clark, and Rosalind E. Clark. 2011. *The Plays*. New York: Scribner. *The Countess Cathleen*.

Yining, Peng. "I Ching: The Book that Helped Translate Itself." *China Daily Europe*, 28 August 2015. http://www.chinadaily.com.cn/a/201508/28/WS5a2b4420a310eefe3e99f3f0.html.

Yu, Jiyuan. "Living with Nature: Stoicism and Daoism." *History of Philosophy Quarterly* 25, no. 1 (2008): 1–19.

Ziporyn, Brook. *Zhuangzi: The Complete Writings*. Indianapolis; Cambridge: Hackett Publishing Company, Inc., 2020.

Zukav, Gary. *The Dancing Wu Li Masters: An Overview of the New Physics*. New York: Quill, 1979.

# INDEX

Page numbers in italics refer to footnotes.

# ABOUT THE AUTHOR

**MAX LANDSBERG** is an internationally recognized authority on personal development, leadership, motivation and executive coaching.

He is an award-winning author, and his eight books have sold more than a million copies in 15 languages. His books all remain in print, including *The Tao of Coaching*, published in 1996, which has become a classic guide to coaching.

Max's books draw on his expertise in strategy, from his time as a Partner at McKinsey & Company; insights into leadership gained as a Senior Partner at two global head-hunting firms, and skills in personal development through private practice as an executive coach. He most recently led McKinsey's Senior Partners Office for seven years.

Max was a Scholar at Cambridge University, and graduated with an MA in Natural Sciences, majoring in Mathematical Physics. He holds an MBA from Stanford University, and many psychological qualifications.

He is also passionate about outdoor adventure, having climbed all 282 of Scotland's highest peaks and hiked longer treks including to K2's Base Camp and Throneroom of the Gods. His other passion – a commitment to the education of the less-privileged – led him to serve as a Governor of Roehampton University for 6 years. Max lives in London, England.

## ALSO BY MAX LANDSBERG

*The Tao of Coaching*
*The Tao of Motivation*
*The Tools of Leadership*
*Mastering Coaching*
*The Call of the Mountains*
*Trek to Everest*
*The Ridgeway*
*The Land's End Circuit*